Christmas Moments

50 Inspirational Stories of the True Meaning of Christmas

COMPILED AND EDITED BY YVONNE LEHMAN

BROKEN ARROW, OK

Unless otherwise noted, all Scripture references are taken from King James Version of the Bible.

Scripture quotations marked NIV are taken from the The Holy Bible, New International Version. Copyright © 1973, 1978, 1984, International Bible Society. Used by permission of Zondervan. All rights reserved.

Scripture quotations marked NASB are taken from the New American Standard Bible®, © Copyright 1960, 1962, 1963, 1968, 1971, 1972, 1973, 1975, 1977 The Lockman Foundation. Used by permission.

Scripture quotations marked NLT are taken from the Holy Bible, New Living Translation, copyright © 1996. Used by permission of Tyndale House Publishers, Inc., Wheaton, Illinois 60189. All rights reserved.

Christmas Moments

50 Inspirational Stories of the True Meaning of Christmas

ISBN-13: 978-1-60495-010-6

ISBN-10: 1-60495-010-2

Copyright © 2014 by Yvonne Lehman. Published in the USA by Grace Publishing. All rights reserved. No part of this book may be reproduced in any form or by any electronic or mechanical means, including information storage and retrieval systems, without permission in writing, except as provided by USA Copyright law.

From Samaritan's Purse

We so appreciate you donating royalties from the sale of the books *Divine Moments* and *Christmas Moments* to Samaritan's Purse. What a blessing that you would think of us! Thank you for your willingness to bless others and bring glory to God through your literary talents. Grace and peace to you.

Their mission statement:

Samaritan's Purse is a nondenominational evangelical Christian organization providing spiritual and physical aid to hurting people around the world.

Since 1970, Samaritan's Purse has helped victims of war, poverty, natural disasters, disease, and famine with the purpose of sharing God's love through his son, Jesus Christ.

Go and do likewise. (Luke 10:37d)

You can find out more by visiting their website at www.samaritanspurse.org.

Dedication

Dedicated to
Terri Kalfas, who saw the beauty
and value of sharing praise in
Divine Moments
and now makes it possible
for the sharing of special
Christmas Moments

and

to the writers who were so eager to share

and

to the readers we hope and pray will be blessed
by our stories as they were with
our first Moments collection

Contents

Introduction 7
1. Where Jesus Walked, *Yvonne Lehman* 9
2. Bethlehem Was Never as Miserable as This!, *Gigi Graham* 16
3. Beneath the Cross, *Edie G. Melson* 19
4. The Gift, *Dr. Rhett H. Wilson, Sr.* 21
5. A Double Blessing on Christmas Eve, *Ann Tatlock* 24
6. A Christmas Point of View, *Vicki H. Moss* 26
7. A Bell Ringer's Epiphany, *Linda Wood Rondeau* 31
8. The Christmas Tree Story, *David Knox Barker* 34
9. Angels in the Snow, *Lydia E. Harris* 40
10. Dreading Christmas, *Janice S. Garey* 42
11. A Christmas Lesson, *Hannah Alexander* 45
12. The Red Birds, *Kimberly Pickens* 47
13. A Night Wrapped in Song, *Lydia E. Harris* 50
14. No Need to Fear Falling, *Vicki H. Moss* 53
15. Snowflake Party, *Deborah Raney* 57
16. Noel, The Cat Who Came for Christmas, *Linda Wood Rondeau* 59
17. The Amazing Gift, *Joann M. Claypoole* 61
18. The Christmas Babies, *Dr. Julie Hale Maschhoff* 65
19. Afraid of Christmas, *Lillian Humphries* 66
20. The Christmas Blanket, *Lori Marett* 69
21. The Fruitcake Caper, *Lydia E. Harris* 72
22. What I Didn't Want for Christmas, *Penny A. Bragg* 74
23. The Miracle Tree, *Linda Wood Rondeau* 76
24. Granny's Dishes, *Gail Griner Golden* 80
25. Christmas Treat, *Yvonne Lehman* 83
26. A Christmas to Remember, *Gigi Graham* 85
27. Christmas Hopes and Fears, *Lydia E. Harris* 90

28. An Unforgettable Christmas Eve, *Alice Klies* 92
29. The Best Christmas Ever, *Tommy Scott Gilmore, III* 95
30. Where Did Prince Charming Go?, *Linda Wood Rondeau* 98
31. My Favorite Childhood Christmas, *Delores Liesner* 100
32. A Partridge in a Pear Tree? The Meaning of a Christmas Carol, *Anonymous* 103
33. A Comedy of Errors, *Gary L. Breezeel* 105
34. Never an Angel, *Colleen L. Reece* 111
35. No Money, No Christmas, *Max Elliot Anderson* 113
36. Christmas 1952, *Toni Armstrong Sample* 117
37. Meeting Jesus at the Toilet Bowl, *Sherry Schumann* 121
38. Christmas Watercolor, *Joann M. Claypoole* 124
39. Having a Blue, Blue Christmas, *Linda Wood Rondeau* 127
40. A is the Answer, *Fran Lee Strickland* 129
41. The Gift of a Lifetime, *Lydia E. Harris* 132
42. The Spirit of Christmas, *John Kincaid* 135
43. Christmas Lights, *Yvonne Lehman* 137
44. Remembering Christmas, *Sharon J. Morris* 138
45. Home for Christmas, *Eric Wiggin* 141
46. A Season of Joy, *Susan Dollyhigh* 144
47. My After-Christmas Surprise, *Lydia E. Harris* 149
48. Gregg's Christmas Eve, *Nate Stevens* 151
49. The First Christmas Without Dad, *Stephanie Grace Whitson* 154
50. Small Things, *Yvonne Lehman* 157
About the Authors 159

❧ Introduction ❧

> What if Christmas doesn't come from a store.
> What if Christmas...perhaps...means a little bit more!
> — Dr. Seuss, *How the Grinch Stole Christmas*

Most likely, you already know, as do the authors of these stories, that there's no "perhaps" to the significance of this holiday season, although the way we celebrate Christmas means much of it may come from a store.

Christmas means not just a little bit...but a lot more!

What prompted us to share a second book in the *Moments* series are the many positive comments about *Divine Moments*, such as the review listed here, written by Lillian Humphries, one of the contributors to that book:

> Through this inspiring book you will find how God is working in our lives daily. With fifty stories written by thirty-seven authors, something will resonate with everyone. *Divine Moments* stories are sweet, humorous, and serious, giving encouragement and hope to all.
>
> *Divine Moments* had its beginning at the Blue Ridge Mountains Christian Writers Conference at the end of a long day when several authors were relaxing and started sharing their personal experiences with God touching their lives.
>
> That evening, Yvonne Lehman began to get the vision for this book. When she put out the call for stories it was obvious that this compilation was meant to be. Stories came flooding in showing God's hand in people's lives. So pay attention to those Divine Moments in your life.

As Lillian mentioned, many did "pay attention" and some authors of stories in *Divine Moments* have contributed to Christmas moments, along with many new authors. I'm delighted about the entertainment and encouragement readers received in that first book and with the enthusiasm of authors contributing to this one with their special Christmas memories.

I've heard it said that a moment may last only a part of a second, but the memory may live on forever.

Someone else said it this way: "Life gives us brief moments with another... but sometimes in those brief moments we get memories that last a lifetime."

Some of the memories in this book range from serious, sad, funny, entertaining, inspiring, encouraging, to lessons learned or just memories of Christmas for some reason important to the writer. All point to the best reason for the Christmas season...celebration of Jesus' birthday!

We wish you, the reader, comfort and joy and the spirit of a Merry Christmas as you experience Christmas Moments in these stories and in your life.

Just as they did in *Divine Moments*, the authors of these articles have generously donated their time and stories. They knew they would receive no monetary compensation but they have experienced what we all do, a sense of peace and joy when we give without expecting anything in return. But, we do expect something because we know God blesses, and in unexpected, wonderful ways. We're already blessed and thrilled that all royalties from the sale of this book will go to a worthy organization, Samaritan's Purse.

~ Yvonne Lehman

❧ 1 ☙

Where Jesus Walked

In 2002 my husband died from cancer. A year later I had cancer. After surgery it appeared that I was cancer-free, but the diagnosis could have been terminal. Those two happenings gave me a greater love for life, and caused me to ask myself what I would do if I could do anything I wanted.

Going to Israel was something I had always wanted to do, but with family, work, and limited finances, such a trip had been out of the question.

Now, I had nothing holding me back.

When I mentioned it to others, the common question was, "Aren't you afraid?"

"No. I'm more afraid of staying home and dying of cancer." I resolved not to let fear hold me back.

I asked two of my children if they wanted to go with me. David said that was his dream. Cindy never dreamed she would have this opportunity. Her husband told her it was the chance of a lifetime and encouraged her to go. His parents helped with the care of their five-year-old son.

I loved the combination – me, my pastor son, and my fun daughter!

I began to pray about it from the moment I thought of going.

David and Cindy prayed.

In my Bible readings, verses and phrases jumped out at me like, "I'll give you the desires of your heart" and "Go to Jerusalem." I don't recall to whom the Lord said those words, but at the time I felt they were being said to me.

The Christmas before we went, with the grandchildren gathered around when I read the biblical account of the birth of Christ, I could say, "Mary and Joseph were from Nazareth. I'm going there. Jesus was born in Bethlehem. I'm going there. I'm going to see the places we read about in the Bible. I'm going to walk on the streets where Jesus walked."

But…I could not even imagine what all I would see, do, learn, and feel.

We made arrangements to go for twelve days in 2004: from February 22–

March 4. We left New York at 7:00 p.m., had a great dinner on the plane, watched movies, took sleeping pills for flying over the Atlantic Ocean, ate a good breakfast, and arrived in Israel at 12:30 p.m. their time.

From the moment I stepped my foot in Israel I felt God's presence in a more profound way than ever before.

We began to walk on the pages of the Bible.

We visited Jaffa (Joppa), where Jonah set sail to flee to Tarshish and away from God's call for him to go to Ninevah.

And Caesarea. The city founded by Herod the Great in 22 BC was the headquarters for Pontius Pilate. South of the town lie ruins of a large Roman theater where Christians were killed or thrown to the lions at the games the Romans held to celebrate the destruction of Jerusalem in AD 70. It was in Caesarea that King Agrippa, after hearing Paul's testimony said, "Almost you persuade me to be a Christian."

We stood on Mount Carmel, the site of Elijah's contest with the 450 prophets of Baal. From there we saw breathtaking views of the entire Jezreel Valley. Overlooking the Valley is the Hill of Megiddo – a name we translate as *Armageddon* – the site of the final struggle between good and evil.

While on the bus we'd look out and see road signs. At home they would have read Asheville, Hendersonville, Marion, Old Fort, Charlotte. These signs read Mount Carmel, Megiddo, Nazareth, Cana, Samaria, Bethlehem.

Nazareth lies in the hills of Galilee, 1,250 feet above sea level about midway between the Sea of Galilee and the Mediterranean Sea. Now the headquarters of the Christian mission movement in Israel, Nazareth is home to dozens of monasteries, churches, convents, orphanages, and private schools. In the days of Jesus, the city was a sleepy, peaceful Galilean town, quite poor, of low reputation and populated by only about 100 families.

In the center of the town is Mary's Well. Seven churches in Nazareth claim to be the place of the angel's announcement of the birth of Jesus to Mary. While we can't be sure of those places, we can be certain that Mary went to this well to draw water, because it's the only natural spring in Nazareth.

We visited Cana, where Jesus performed his first miracle, turning water into wine. Then we went to Tiberias for dinner and ate St. Peter's Fish (served whole on a platter, eyes and all!). Tiberias is at the Sea of Galilee.

We stayed in a kibbutz, a communal settlement where each person works according to his ability and receives all that family's needs. There's no personal wealth and no salary. The first Israeli Kibbutz was established in 1920. During the 1930s, European Jews who saw the coming of the Holocaust went to Israel in large numbers and the kibbutz society was firmly established.

The Sea of Galilee is a beautiful blue. Most of Jesus' teaching and ministry took place in the villages and hills surrounding the sea. Because of a gap in the western mountains where air currents move through rapidly, terrible storms come up quickly and without warning, causing sudden – sometimes violent – changes in the sea. During just such a storm the disciples were terrified… and Jesus calmed the storm.

When I was in a boat on that sea I wasn't afraid, but I did feel like I could walk on water. I didn't try it, though!

Capernaum, once a wealthy and prosperous town, was also the home of high-ranking Roman officials. Jesus performed more of his miracles there than in any other place. Capernaum was the home of Peter and Andrew, James and John. There, archaeologists have uncovered the ruins of one of the most elegant white limestone synagogues in Israel, believed to be the one in which Jesus taught. One of the stones has the Hebrew inscription: "John the son of Zebedee made these stones. May it be for him a blessing."

The lovely Church of Beatitudes is situated on the hillside above Capernaum, overlooking the Sea of Galilee. Tradition has marked it as the site of the Sermon on the Mount. The natural acoustics there would have enabled the crowds to hear distinctly every word Jesus spoke.

My son stood there and read the beatitudes and commented on them. At that moment, I saw him not just as my son, but as my teacher. I realized that at some point Mary saw, and had to accept, that Jesus was not only her son, but also her teacher, her savior.

The Jordan River forms a natural boundary between Israel and opposing nations. It has always played a significant role in biblical history. It is the only river in the world that flows for most of its course below sea level. The living waters of the Jordan flow into the Dead Sea, symbolically carrying sin to where nothing can live, and demonstrating how our sins are removed and forgotten by God through the fact that they no longer exist. My third baptism took place in that river. (My first baptism was as a child, the second as an adult re-commitment.) How special to have been baptized where John the Baptizer baptized Jesus!

The Golan Heights, the border between Israel and Syria, is of great strategic importance. Whoever controls the Golan Heights controls Israel. In May of 1967 Israel served notice on Syria to be prepared to face the consequences of its attacks and encroachments of increasing intensity and frequency against Israel settlements and into the demilitarized zones along the Syrian border. Syria appealed to Egypt and Iraq for aid. War broke out. During the Six-Day War of June 1967, Egypt, Syria, Jordan and Iraq joined forces against Israel. Just as in Old Testament times, God threw the enemy into confusion and they were the agents of their own defeat.

We took a cable car to the top of Masada, Herod's winter home, or palace. Masada is the site of one of the most dramatic episodes in Jewish history. After the fall of Jerusalem in AD 70, a few survivors of that battle joined Jewish zealots at Masada. It became the only outpost to hold out for three years. The tragic AD 73 last stand of the Zealots marked the end of Jewish independence until 1948.

Masada has become a symbol for modern Israel. Now, young Jewish boys hike up the serpentine path and camp out on Masada prior to their Bar Mitzvahs. New recruits in the Israeli Army are given their rifles in a ceremony on the summit of Masada, and take an oath of allegiance to Israel, solemnly swearing, "Masada shall not fall again."

On the western shore of the Dead Sea is the lovely oasis En Gedi. Luxurious vegetation, lovely waterfalls. Its date palms have made it famous for their delicious fruit. The springs of fresh water and caves in the hillsides made En Gedi a natural refuge for David in his flight from Saul.

We walked in that pool and marveled at the water flowing over those rocks. I could imagine David being able to hide among those boulders and see Saul and his army coming for miles across that desert. David could duck behind rocks, go into caves, nourish himself with fruit, and bathe in that waterfall's pool.

What a privilege to visit Jerusalem, the Holy City, chosen by God to be his special dwelling place! Located thirty-eight miles east of the Mediterranean Sea and fourteen miles west of the Dead Sea in "the tops of the mountains," it is beautifully situated about 2,740 feet above sea level.

During the 1948 war for Israeli Independence, the Old City fell to the Arabs, and the Jews were once again banished from all of their holy places. When the Jews captured Old Jerusalem in 1967 during the Six-Day War, the Old City came under Jewish rule for the first time in nineteen centuries. Defense Minister Moshe Dayan said, "We have returned to our holy places, never to part from them again." The old city is divided into four quarters – Jewish, Arab Christian, Moslem, and Armenian — by her two main streets.

The Mount of Olives, named for the olive trees that once grew on its slopes, abounds with Christian shrines marking events of the last days of Jesus on earth. The largest and oldest Jewish cemetery in the world, dating back to biblical times, is located on the Mount of Olives.

Gethsemane, the garden on the lower slopes of the Mount of Olives was apparently a place Jesus visited frequently. Flowers and shrubs grow along the pathway in the well-kept garden, a reminder of beauty in the quiet place where Jesus underwent the most sorrowful hour of his passion. The writings of Josephus tell us in the AD 70 siege of Jerusalem Titus destroyed all the trees within nine miles of Jerusalem. The trees presently growing on the slopes of the Mount of Olives sprouted from the roots of some of those trees. In the Garden of Gethsemane eight gnarled trees stand today. Carbon dating on their roots show they may be as old as 3,000 years.

The Garden of Gethsemane points to the location of the second coming of Jesus.

Many of our tour group cried constantly. I think I was too overcome with disbelief that I was really walking in the pages of the Bible, experiencing the closeness of God's Spirit so profoundly, seeing places I'd been taught about for so many years. That changed when we were in the courtyard outside Caiaphas' house, the place where Jesus was led from Gethsemane on the night of his arrest. A statue of Peter stands in the courtyard, because that's where he denied Jesus. I could not hold back my flood of tears, so aware was I that sins against Jesus aren't only acts of commission, but omission, neglect, and complacency. When we sat on the steps, undisputedly walked on by Jesus, we sang hymns. Below us a group of Koreans sang hymns in their language. I was reminded of the song "When We All Get to Heaven."

The Western Wall, the holiest shrine of the Jewish world, is a portion of the wall built by Herod, and all that's left of the temple. It's sixty yards long and sixty feet high. Since the return of the Jews in 1967, the wall has not been abandoned for a single moment; prayers are offered there constantly. I felt particularly privileged to write down a prayer request and place it in a crevice of the wall.

Via Dolorosa, meaning "Way of Sorrow" or "Way of the Cross" is the pathway on which Jesus carried the cross. We walked along those same stones.

Many Christians consider the hill of Calvary or Golgotha (The Skull) the most sacred place on earth. West of Golgotha is the Garden tomb, fitting the descriptions of a rock-hewn tomb. It's entered through a door in a large rock wall, and is composed of two chambers, one for mourning, the other for burial couches. There's a deep groove at the front of the tomb for securing a large stone as a closure. It's often noted that the tomb was opened not so Jesus could get out, but so the world could get in, and see, "He is not here. He is risen."

Our group took communion at the Garden tomb. I can't imagine a more perfect place for communion than while facing the tomb like the one – or perhaps the exact one – from which Jesus arose.

Several nights we went underground in the stone tunnels that run underneath Israel. We saw Hezekiah's tunnel and cisterns.

We visited the Yad Vasheem, the Jewish Holocaust memorial museum, where candles burn continuously and on Yom Hashoah – Holocaust Martyrs' and Heroes' Remembrance Day – names are read for the six million Jews who died in the Holocaust.

Palestinians controlled Bethlehem, six miles south of Jerusalem. When our original trip to Bethlehem was cancelled because of possible danger, we feared we wouldn't get to see where Jesus was born. However, the trip was rescheduled.

We couldn't go in on buses, but had to take cabs. We had to show our passports. We were met and guarded by Palestinians in military uniform, carrying their weapons.

To our great relief (although not knowing if we'd be allowed to leave!) we went inside the magnificent Church of the Nativity, built by Constantine in AD 330 over the cave stable which is believßed to have been the place of Jesus' birth. We were allowed to shop in the Bethlehem stores, but not have a worship service.

But we found the perfect place for a worship service and to celebrate Jesus' birth after we learned that shepherds still pasture their flocks in the fields around Bethlehem. We stood in Shepherd's Field, above which the angels appeared in the sky and announced and sang to the shepherds about Jesus' birth. As darkness fell, we lit candles and sang hymns, carols, and of course, "O Little Town of Bethlehem."

That year at Christmas I could tell my grandchildren I saw what Jesus saw. I walked on the streets where he walked. I rode in a boat on the Sea of Galilee where Jesus walked on water. I saw the place where he was crucified. I went inside an empty tomb like the one in which he was buried. I saw the mountain from which he ascended into the heavens.

I want to go back to Israel, to feel that special closeness to God again, knowing I'm around his chosen people and in the land he loves so dearly. I want to see the 1,500-year-old church they've recently uncovered.

That trip was a blessed experience of a lifetime. I'm so grateful I could go, and visit with my son and daughter.

All that – and more – are reasons I want to go back.

Oh yes, one more thing. I want to ride that camel again!

~ Yvonne Lehman

~ 2 ~

Bethlehem Was Never as Miserable as This!

The Christmas season had arrived again, brimming with joy and anticipation. But there was also the usual hustle and bustle of all the preparations – shopping, wrapping, decorating, and baking.

Finally everything was ready. We all loaded into the car and drove to my parents' home in North Carolina. That first glimpse of "home" always fuels our excitement and anticipation. It's almost as though we can smell the fresh apple pie and feel the warmth of a cozy fire before we get out of the car.

This excitement built to a crescendo on Christmas Eve as each child and adult hung his or her stocking from the fireplace mantle in the large living room. With a twinkle in his eye, Daddy gathered all of us around and placed a long distance call to Santa at the North Pole – just to make sure he'd received all the children's gift lists and to wish him a speedy trip.

As we tucked the children into bed, the unmistakable sound of sleigh bells jingled somewhere over the roof of the house. (My brother had hung donkey bells on the chimney.) Needless to say, sleep didn't come easily for the children that night!

When Christmas morning arrived everyone rushed downstairs. A fire blazed merrily on the hearth, and the aroma of coffee and sweet rolls met us in the kitchen. By strict family tradition, no one was allowed into the living room where the Christmas tree stood guard over the bulging stockings and brightly wrapped gifts until after breakfast.

The children quickly inhaled a few bites and then sat waiting as patiently as possible. Finally the last drop of coffee was downed and the eager faces of the children turned for the anticipated permission to rush into the living room.

But Daddy decided to have devotions first. He announced that he would read the Christmas story. The children accepted this with a few audible sighs.

Then after the story and prayer, they jumped up out of their seats. But once again they were disappointed. This time, my sister Anne said she wanted the children to line up and enter the living room one by one so she could take pictures.

That did it! My young son turned to his grandmother and said with utter exasperation and disgust, "Bethlehem was never as miserable as this!"

Later, smiling as I recalled my son's remark, I remembered another Christmas Eve. I recalled sitting on the floor with tears of exhaustion streaking down my cheeks as I wrapped gifts until long past midnight. My smile faded as I remembered just how miserable I'd felt that night.

Something has happened to our holiday season that often makes it seem more of a burden than a blessing.

Have you ever wondered how that first Christmas Eve might have been celebrated? Were the cherubim and the seraphim, angels of every description, hurriedly preparing to send the Lord of heaven down to earth in the form of a baby boy?

Perhaps on one side of heaven angels were working on the magnificent program they would present to the shepherds. Another angel might have been arranging to send that special star sailing across the skies to eventually guide the wise men to the little Messiah. Maybe another angel tenderly watched over Joseph and Mary as they made their way toward the stable.

Of course we don't know exactly what happened, but we do know that when all was ready, *God sent forth his Son.* (Galatians 4:4) And all of heaven gathered as the King of kings and the Lord of lords laid aside his glory, placing it at his Father's feet and saying, *"A body hast thou prepared me....Lo, I come... to do thy will, O God."* (Hebrews 10:5, 7)

While the heavenly preparations might have been complex, the earthly men and women involved in the first Christmas kept it simple.

The hearts of a few willing people – Mary, Joseph, the shepherds, and the wise men – were simple. The site of the birth, a small stable in a small town, was simple. The celebration was simple: Shepherds, hard-working men, left their work for a few hours to go and "see this thing which [had] come to pass." (Luke 2:15) And then they returned to their responsibilities.

The gifts were also simple, yet their value was priceless, timeless, and eternal:
- Joseph gave his obedience.
- Mary gave her body.
- The shepherds gave their adoration.

There were those who missed that first Christmas altogether.
- The innkeeper was too busy with the mundane cares of his guests.
- The guests themselves were too concerned with bodily comforts and personal affairs to be bothered with happenings in the stable.
- King Herod was too absorbed with his insecurities, his court, and his pathetic dreams of glory.

They were all too busy, too concerned, too wrapped up in other things.

I began asking myself whether I had almost missed Christmas. Have I been too busy, too preoccupied with material concerns and what others might think if things are not "just right"? Am I in danger of missing the real meaning of Christmas? I don't think for a moment the Lord would have us dampen the excitement of Christmas. After all, He himself has given us "all things to enjoy." (1 Timothy 6:17)

Perhaps this year our Christmas lists should read:
- More attention to our toddlers
- More time and appreciation for our parents and our mates
- More unconditional acceptance of our teenagers
- More love and concern for our friends

And what about our gift to the One whose birthday we celebrate? All he asks is the gift of ourselves – with all our faults and failures, problems and fears. This is Christmas.

God giving,
our receiving,
God fulfilling.
Blessed Christmas!

~ Gigi Graham

3

Beneath the Cross

One Christmas I found myself huddled beneath the cross where Jesus hung dying.

Now, this may seem a bit farfetched. But for those of you who know me, it's not quite as strange as it seems. I love the theater. I even majored in costume design for a time in college. But now my favorite theater is found in the church. Being involved in church dramas gives me a new perspective on the stories of the Bible. It just seems to come to life when it's being portrayed on the stage.

Yet as much as I love being a part of the production, I do not like being an actor. I absolutely hate being in front of a large group of people. I've found my place, though. My enjoyment is fulfilled by being part of the stage crew. Specifically, I love helping the actors with props and wardrobe…and that's exactly how I came to be kneeling at the foot of the cross.

My job that year was to assist the actor who portrayed Jesus. I'd been assigned to help him get up on the cross while the stage was darkened. It had been erected high up, in the baptistery. But because of the stage design, once I'd helped him get settled and secure, I didn't have time to get off stage. To stay out of the audience's sight, I had to huddle in a tight crouch, just inches away from the massive wooden cross. During the rehearsals the actor and I laughed about the fact that I was stuck there for several minutes.

Then came the first night of performances.

I helped the actor onto the cross and took my kneeling position. Even though I was dressed in black from head to toe, I made myself as small as possible so I wouldn't draw the audience's attention and detract from the crucifixion scene. But as I crouched there, the circumstances around me seemed to change. The groans and writhing of the actor on the cross became those of Jesus. Watching the crowd of actors below, I heard their cries and felt my heart chilled by their impassive faces as they observed the drama.

Was this the way it had been two thousand years ago? The question in my mind transported me fully to ancient Jerusalem as my heart flooded with parallels. I was no longer taking part in just a drama on stage. Jesus' agony and sacrifice became real in a way I could never have imagined.

The black I wore was no longer just a necessary uniform. It represented my sin and my invisibility to God in my wretchedness.

My silence, while necessary and expected during the performance, stung me with the resemblance of real life. The world expects me to be silent about the cross, or at least speak of it in a tasteful way so it doesn't offend anyone. And so often I had complied and remained quiet instead of speaking out.

Finally, my ability to remain hidden from the audience and melt into the background reminded me that while the world might not see me as I really am, Jesus had a perfect view of me while he hung suffering.

Yes, that Christmas I found myself huddled at the base of the cross where Jesus hung dying.

And I will never be the same.

The word of the cross is foolishness to those who are perishing, but to us who are being saved it is the power of God.
1 Corinthians 1:18 (NASB)

~ Edie Melson

❧ 4 ❧

The Gift

My wife says there is only one day of the year that I enjoy shopping – and she's right. I love shopping for my family the day after Thanksgiving. So, one Black Friday I hurried among the many shoppers scurrying to Kmart, Westgate Mall, and dozens of other stores in Spartanburg, South Carolina.

While shopping at the Christian Supply bookstore early that Friday morning, I noticed the attractive burgundy, leather-bound *One Year Bible*. These Bibles contained daily readings taking the reader through the entire Scriptures in one year. While admiring them, I thought of the small group I'd started earlier that year in our church. A dozen men gathered early each Thursday morning for breakfast, prayer, and Bible study. The Lord seemed to bless the group, and the men desired to grow spiritually.

I sensed a prompting from the Holy Spirit to purchase one of those Bibles for each of the men in our prayer group.

I was an associate pastor at a rural church; money was never plentiful. We had a two-year old at home, and our second child was due in about four weeks. The Bibles were on sale that day for $20.00 each. I quickly did the math and figured that one Bible for each of twelve men totaled $240.00.

Earlier that week, the church had given Christmas bonuses to the staff. My Christmas bonus was $250.00. Now it seemed the Lord wanted me to give all of the money back to Him.

Thinking and quieting my spirit, I prayed, "Father, if you are leading me in this venture, I will trust and obey you." I purchased the Bibles, another addition to my Black Friday treasures.

The following Monday at work, the church's financial secretary entered my office and announced, "I just discovered we made an error this year with your family's insurance payments. We owe you a refund."

She handed me a check for $250.00.

The next couple of years, watching the men use their Bibles regularly brought me satisfaction. Coupled with that was the joy of knowing how God had provided. He had given, urged me to give, and given to me again.

Eight years later I was learning anew to look to God as my Source and trust him for the needs of my family. We believed God was leading us to take a huge step of faith. I felt led to resign from my current position, but had no other job lined up.

While attending an October prayer retreat at Ridgecrest Conference Center, I stretched out facedown on the cement slab of a shelter my children used during summer camp. I prayed, "Lord, I have no idea how I am going to provide for my family. Christmas is coming, and I have no money for Christmas presents for them. But Father, if I know you are leading us, I will step out and obey you." The Father confirmed that day to my wife and me to move forward, and I resigned that afternoon – a scary move.

I told no one my fear of not having money for Christmas presents.

One month later, a friend took me to lunch. When I left the restaurant, he followed me to my car, put his hand on my shoulder, and said, "Rhett, I believe you have obeyed the Lord and I respect you for stepping out in faith. I know that Christmas is coming, and you want to bless your children. I just want you to know that I support you as you follow God."

With joy on his face, he handed me a sealed envelope. After he left and I opened it, I found he had given me $1,000 in cash.

My former church understood too, that I was stepping out in faith. They graciously compensated me for several months after my resignation. By the time that provision ended, I was working in my new position of planting a new church.

Life continues to hold challenges for my wife and me of trusting in God's financial provision. We work. We give. We try and spend wisely. We trust God to care for us. And we continue learning the lesson that we can depend on the God who sees us and knows our needs both today and tomorrow.

Each Christmas, in particular, I'm reminded of God's provision when I think of the need of Mary and Joseph. God sent wise men bringing valuable gifts. Those treasures of gold, frankincense, and myrrh could be used to barter and help the holy family in the long months before they returned to Nazareth. God knew the need and provided.

As I sit with my family and exchange gifts, I think of my friend who gave me that $1,000 at Christmastime. He understood that presents are not what bring the most joy, rather it is the act of giving and receiving. And I thank God for the greatest gift – his Son. He just wants us to receive.

– Dr. Rhett H. Wilson

❧ 5 ❧
A Double Blessing on Christmas Eve

The young man's debit card wouldn't work, leaving him stranded at the cash register in the grocery store.

"And you don't take credit cards?" he asked the cashier.

"No. Sorry," she said.

"Checks?"

"Only cash or debit."

He tried the debit card several more times, with no success. Finally, looking dejected, he said, "I guess I'll have to put everything back."

"Sorry," the cashier said again, although she didn't sound sorry at all. Due to the store's strict payment policy, she had no doubt seen this scenario before.

I was the customer in line right behind him. As I watched the scene play out, I kept thinking I ought to step in and pay for this man's groceries.

But I didn't. I was afraid. Afraid that if I bought his groceries today, I wouldn't have the money I needed to buy my own family's groceries next week.

The young man pushed the cart back into the store to unload everything he had collected. I paid for my items and left the store annoyed with myself. "Forgive me, Lord," I prayed inwardly. "I have a feeling you were nudging me, and I didn't obey. Next time this happens, I will pay for the person's groceries while trusting you to provide for my own family."

The next time it happened was late in the afternoon on Christmas Eve. I was picking up a few last-minute items with my twelve-year-old daughter Laura.

When we got in line to check out, the scene was already underway. Only this time the woman couldn't find her debit card and she didn't have enough cash. "And you don't take credit cards?"

"No. Sorry."

She fumbled nervously through her purse and wallet, seeking the elusive debit card. From the look on her tired face, I could tell life was not easy for her. In fact, I could well imagine that every day was a financial struggle. And here she was, trying to find a way to pay for what looked like her family's Christmas dinner. Her fingers trembled as she muttered, "I'll have to put everything back."

"I'll pay for hers," I hollered to the cashier as I started unloading my own groceries. "Just ring my items up and I'll pay for hers with mine."

Two pairs of startled eyes turned to me, and for a moment, both the woman and the cashier balked. But I insisted. The woman bagged her groceries while I paid. When she finished, she threw her arms around me in a tight hug.

"Thank you," she said. "I hope Santa Claus will be good to you!"

Hugging her in return, I assured her it was the Lord who had already been good to me, and I was glad to share the blessing with her.

While I was bagging my own groceries, I could see her through the glass door of the grocery store. She was outside talking with a young boy I thought could be her grandson. He looked at me, looked at his grandmother, looked back at me.

When Laura and I stepped outside, he greeted us with a huge smile and shining eyes. "Merry Christmas!" he said.

"Merry Christmas!" Laura and I chimed together.

When we got in the car, Laura turned to me and said, "Mom, you're my hero."

A double blessing! I was able to keep my promise to the Lord by helping someone, and Laura was able to witness the love of Christ in action on Christmas Eve.

- Ann Tatlock

∂ 6 ∽

A Christmas Point of View

I was in Denver for Christmas celebrations with family, watching the red velvet cake beckon from its white cake stand while sides for the ham were well on their way to bubbling perfection in the oven, when I received a phone call.

John "Jack" Koblas, a writer/poet friend, wished me a Merry Christmas and asked what I'd been up to. He cared nothing for my talk about attending church that morning to celebrate the upcoming birthday of Jesus. He claimed to be an agnostic who hadn't prayed since his grandmother died after he'd begged God to heal her when he was a child. A lonely man angry at God was putting it mildly.

"If you want to keep talking with me you'd better stop talking about that religious stuff," he warned.

Although laughing at his gruff jab, I had to give him credit for his past accomplishments. Having written over seventy books, Koblas was a Minnesota historian and authority when it came to Jesse and Frank James and the Cole–Younger gang's last robbery attempt in Minnesota.

He'd been a consultant and scriptwriter for various TV documentaries including History Channel, PBS American Experience, Discovery Channel, as well as independent film companies. His 1950s rock n' roll doo-wop band, The Magpies, had also been inducted into the Minnesota Rock and Country Hall of Fame. His lifetime accomplishments were many.

Of course he had no way of knowing I wasn't impressed with celebrities and rock stars because I knew the true Rock Star, and when I finally contained my laughter I said, "Well Jacko, the rocks would cry out if I stopped talking about Jesus, God, and what all He's done for me. And if you want to keep talking with me, you'll have to keep hearing about it."

Some may wonder how I, a conservative Southern Christian writer from the Tennessee portion of the Bible Belt, became friends with an agnostic writer from Minneapolis, Minnesota, who was steeped in socialism with serious issues when it came to "caps" – what he called capitalists.

The answer is Facebook. The internet isn't a total waste of time.

When Jack sent me a friend request, I checked him out through his wall conversations to make sure he was legit and not a slasher. Surely he couldn't have had so many people replying to his updates about the ravages of Parkinson's disease and other health ailments if his claims weren't true.

I checked out Jack's books on Amazon to verify he was an author and historian and discovered the man was who he claimed to be. His photos matched up with book back flaps – although he wrote under the name of John Koblas.

He'd also written six books on F. Scott Fitzgerald and Sinclair Lewis. But there was one book that had been made into a documentary that caught my attention – *The Jesse James Northfield Raid: Confessions of the Ninth Man*. Intrigued by Jesse James since I was a child – I used to watch a TV show about the notorious outlaw – I ordered the book. What I read on page three mesmerized me, and I messaged Jack.

Later, we had a phone conversation. "Jack," I questioned. "Don't you think it incredible what happened with Bill Stiles, the so-called ninth man who was holding horses for the robbery getaway and escaped? Later, when trying to avoid the law, he ducked into a service at the Union Rescue Mission in Los Angeles and was convicted by the Holy Spirit!"

Jack gave a grunt, basically unresponsive. Rushing on with my excitement, I ignored Jack's lack of enthusiasm about spiritual matters. "Stiles had the 'soup' or nitroglycerin in his hotel room while trying to scope out his next robbery and when the evangelist, Mel Trotter, asked him to give himself to God, Stiles claimed he didn't believe in God because of the horrible lifestyle he had been forced to live. Then when he tried to stand up to leave, he found he had no control over his legs."

Since Jack wasn't interrupting me, I kept on. "Let me read what you wrote while quoting Stiles." I read what Jack had written:

> "I do not know what you think," recalled the outlaw, "but I know my legs were fastened to the floor by a power not of this earth. I kept trying to get up, when a woman came and sat down beside

me, and urged me to go up to the altar. I listened to her pleadings for a time and then consented to go, thinking it would do me no harm anyway.

"What seemed so strange to me was that I did not have any power to resist. It was not the woman, for I had been a woman-hater since my early life; it was the power of God. As soon as I gave my consent my legs were released, and I went up and knelt at the altar."

"Jack," I said, "don't you think that's remarkable. Stiles was so convicted by the Holy Spirit that he wept until he converted to Christianity from a life of hard crime? Didn't this blow you away when you first researched it?"

Jack remained silent about the subject, so I pursued it no longer.

After Christmas, on the airplane flying home from Denver, I could see the ground below when I heard in my spirit, "Call Jack." Strange. At this point in our friendship we were only talking about once a week, and I hadn't expected to hear from him for several days. Whenever he would call, we'd catch up on the writing life, life in general, and exchange our points of view.

The plane was circling to land. I couldn't call right at that moment. I thought I'd wait until Thursday for his call.

Then I heard again in my spirit, "Call Jack as soon as you get off the plane."

Detailed this time. There was an urgency to these messages, but as usual I was thinking "Where is this coming from?" Reasoning it had to be from God because the devil would gloat if we all dropped dead and went to hell, I mumbled, "Lord, can't I wait until I find my luggage and get on the road?"

No more messages. Good. I'd wait. While gathering my bags, I had a nagging feeling that something was wrong, but what could I do from Tennessee?

Buckled into the seat of my car, I made the phone call and someone picked up the phone. "Jack?"

No answer. Then a clear click and disconnect.

Now I was worried. Recent snow dumped on Minnesota was serious. Snowdrifts sometimes lasted until May. Jack had shared he'd often thought about the Native American Indian custom of dealing with evident death by leaving the tribe for higher ground to die alone. Since he knew his time was short with so many health issues and he couldn't easily make it to higher ground – after ten years of dealing with his disease he often fell backward and sometimes struggled to eat and walk – he'd decided getting lost in a snowdrift might be a viable solution.

I called again and left a message. "Just calling to make sure you haven't ambled outside and wandered into a snow drift. If you're in a snow drift and have your phone with you listening to this message, call me back."

Two minutes later, my phone rang. "I'm ov…overwhelmed."

"Jack?"

"I'm…I'm overwhelmed."

"You're not in a snowdrift are you? What's wrong? Don't make me come up there with a shovel! You need for me to call an ambulance?"

I tried to use humor to cheer him while offering to make phone calls. There were times when Jack had trouble getting himself into bed. His muscles mutinied and refused to cooperate with his mind. His entire body seemed to shut down. Hallucinations were frequent from twenty medications he managed to swallow. During rough morning times, when he'd been without meds from sleeping through the night and the Parkinson's ran through his veins like a freight train jumping track, he'd manage to hit the speed dial button. Once our connection had been made, I'd try to coax him through each dilemma. Living in a nursing home was out of the question. He'd decided to tough it out at home alone.

"No, I'm fine."

"You don't sound fine."

"No. I'm not fine. I was having a really bad day. Everything was getting to me. I just needed to talk with you. You always make me laugh. I finally called out and said, 'God, I can't take this anymore. I need to talk with Vicki right now. If there really is a God and you are who you say you are – if you're out there – have her call me. Now.' You called within five minutes. I'm…I'm overwhelmed."

Relieved his problem was emotional and spiritual and not extremely physical at the moment, I was delighted God was working in this man's life. "Yes, well I was being given some orders while I was on the plane to call you as soon as I landed. Do you believe God is alive and well now, Jacko?"

Humbled, Jack replied, "He has to be. Or else, how could this happen? This is no coincidence, this has to be of God."

"I think you're right. And he's a God who loves giving gifts." I couldn't help but laugh with joy. "Merry Christmas, Jack."

~ *Vicki H. Moss*

The rest of the story…

Believing-prayer works. I also believe God brings certain people into the paths of others to help us through our travels before we journey home. Before Jack and I met on Facebook, I'd shared with a friend that I was too busy to date anyone but it would be nice to have a guy writer friend to be able to discuss writing – from a man's point of view.

Two weeks later, Jack and I were discussing the writing life and soon began a writing project together that has yet to be published. After many more conversations of a spiritual nature and delving into the Bible, I walked Jack through the sinner's prayer. Tears poured down his face, just as they had Bill Stiles', the outlaw he wrote about.

After accepting the Lord Jesus Christ as his Savior, Jack lived three more years, passing into the arms of Jesus in 2013. One day I hope to meet up with him again to enjoy hearing about his latest point of view.

❧ 7 ☙

A Bell Ringer's Epiphany

Why had I volunteered when I had so many things to do? The cold gets into my bones until nothing can make me feel warm again. But I had offered to be a bell ringer for the Salvation Army's Christmas drive. So I bundled up and trekked to my station at the local grocery store, donned the apron and picked up the emblem of my assignment – a small golden handbell.

One by one, people came up to the little red bucket and dropped in coins or bills. Sometimes people stopped and chatted. Some nodded and left. Still others dropped their gift and scurried off to complete other tasks the season required of them.

"I brought you here to teach you something," the Spirit said to my heart.

Not to be so quick to volunteer?

"No. I want you to study these people. Examine the way they give."

And, I did. To my amazement, I learned the reasons for giving are as varied as the people who donate. Then I began to see similarities in people's motivation. And, I wondered where my heart would fit among theirs.

I listened to a lady who gave from her sorrow. This was her first Christmas without her mother. Her father had passed away only a year before. Eyes brimming with tears, she pushed twenty dollars into the bucket. "My mother was a bell ringer," she said. "Thank you for doing this." Then she rushed off, uncomfortable with her emotions.

The Spirit spoke again: *He was despised and rejected by men, a man of sorrows, and familiar with suffering.* (Isaiah 52:3)

A man, exuding wealth, approached the kettle. He wore stone-washed jeans over high-fashion boots. His leather designer coat gleamed in the winter sun. He plopped a ten-dollar bill down, huffing with pride over a gift that appeared to be hardly a sacrifice. Though he gave from his abundance, the effort cost him little.

The Spirit spoke again: *From everyone who has been given much, much will be demanded: and from the one who has been entrusted with much, much more will be asked.* (Luke 12:48)

An elderly woman approached. Her threadbare coat and frayed scarf indicated her station in life. Her cart also bore testament to her poverty. She stopped before the red kettle, pulled out a thin and worn wallet from her purse, and dropped in her last two coins. "Maybe this will bring me good fortune," she said. She gave from her need, as if investing into generosity would bring better days.

The Spirit spoke yet again: *My God will meet all your needs according to his glorious riches in Christ Jesus.* (Philippians 4:19)

Another elderly woman stopped by the kettle. Her head drooped from her heavy burden. She shrugged her shoulders then reached into her purse for an assortment of change. "I don't feel right if I pass by one of these drums and give nothing." She trotted off, head slightly higher. Her giving well was a fountain of guilt.

The Spirit spoke anew: *I know my transgressions, and my sin is always before me.* (Psalm 51:3)

Last, a young man eagerly approached the drum in a manner much akin to Tigger's Happy Bounce, and tossed in his coins with a whistle. "I love this!" he said as he sailed out the door. "God's been good to me. This is one way I can say, 'Thank you.'" The young man gave from gratitude.

The Spirit spoke once more then fell silent: *Each man should give what he has decided in his heart to give, not reluctantly or under compulsion, for God loves a cheerful giver.* (1 Corinthians 9:7)

Then I understood what the Holy Spirit wanted me to learn. Christmas is a time of giving.

I analyzed my own motivations. Do I give grudgingly because it's expected? Do I donate from a feeling of loss? Do I hope one day my giving will be multiplied? Do I fear what will happen if I do not give?

The little bell rang for me as well, and I am grateful for what God taught me that day. I had entered the experience full of pride that I was doing something for God. Yet, He did far more for me in the lesson I learned: True giving springs from a grateful heart.

God so loved the world, that he gave his only begotten Son, that whosoever believeth in him should not perish, but have everlasting life. (John 3:16)

~ Linda Wood Rondeau

8

The Christmas Tree Story

Corrie gazed out the picture window. Snowflakes were piling up on the old stone wall. The light atop the ivy-covered wrought-iron lamppost by the walkway grew dim, obscured by heavy snowfall. It was Christmas Eve. All around the world, excited children anxiously awaited the arrival of Christmas Day. But for Corrie and her brother, Kevin, it seemed they simply waited. Even the old grandfather clock in the hall took an extra long pause between the tick…and the tock.

A white Christmas was in store, but they were not thinking of snowmen. Presents were not on their minds.

Their mother was very sick. She could not participate in preparing for the Christmas season as she had in years past. Piling into the car with mother and father and going to get the tree had always been the Christmas season kickoff event. Corrie and Kevin had grown accustomed to that favorite family tradition.

But this year, there was no Christmas tree in the family room, the living room, or the playroom. In fact, there was no Christmas tree anywhere in the large old Victorian house on the hill.

That morning, Kevin had told Corrie he'd overheard the doctor saying that their mother would not likely leave her bed again. Corrie had shaken her head and said with great confidence, "But Daddy will find the cure. I have faith in him."

Their father had gone to New York City on business. He and many others were working toward a cure for illnesses like their mother had. After years of medical research, recent progress held promise. Before her father left for New York he had promised that God would help the doctors find the cure in his perfect timing.

Her father had explained that God hears our prayers and can reach into our lives and help whenever he chooses, but he also wants to put his plans into action through us and our work. God doesn't want to do all the work that he has prepared and equipped people to do, he'd said.

Their father had planned to return in time to take them out for the family tradition of picking a tree. But he'd been delayed.

*

Their mother's sense of helplessness made her heart ache for her young children. She struggled with questions of life, purpose, guilt, and hope for her family. Her mind longed for future Christmas seasons. Even now while feeling the precious gift of life slipping away, she longed to see and hold her grandchildren and great-grandchildren.

She had always made Christmas a special time of the year for her family. Baking, cooking, decorating the house and focusing her time and energy on the family were her great passions. She considered that her special role and privilege.

During this Christmas season, her sister and her children attended to their family's needs. It was the hardest thing she had ever done, to just rest in the love and care of others, to be served instead of serving. A deep sadness and sense of loss pulled at her. But she resisted and reminded herself of the wonderful memories she possessed.

*

Finally, the phone had rung and Corrie had talked to her father. He was on his way from the airport. Kevin was excited. "It's going to be a good Christmas after all."

The headlights on their father's car came up the drive and glared through the picture window, silhouetting the large snowflakes like hundreds of angels descending to earth.

"Hooray! Hooray! Daddy's home! It's Christmas tree time!" Corrie shouted, running through the house as the car pulled into the garage.

He hugged and kissed them, then went to see their mother.

Soon, Corrie and Kevin had their jackets, hats and gloves on and stood at the end of their mother's bed. They were ready for the annual tradition of searching for the right tree. Mother's face wore the expression Corrie had seen in years past when she had enjoyed one of the favorite traditions with the family.

But she couldn't go this year.

Corrie and Kevin pressed their noses to the car's cold windows and wondered what tree they would choose. Their father drove past Christmas tree lots that were all closed and empty.

The roads were getting slick with ice and snow. Corrie wondered if they could even get to the place where they always chose the right tree. Finally they came to the weathered old barn. Dangling from a mishmash of old electric cords, dim bulbs lighted the small lot next to the barn. However, the lot looked as empty as those closed ones in town.

As snow crunched under the tires as the car pulled to a stop, a rather gruff looking man in coveralls and a tattered work coat hung a sign on the old barn door. Closed for Christmas. The lights flickered off.

"Oh, no!" Corrie moaned. "We're too late."

They jumped out of the car and rushed up to the Christmas tree man. Corrie reached him first. "Please sir, please! You can't be closed. We've come to pick out our Christmas tree."

"Sorry," he said. "I sold the last one five minutes ago."

"Don't you have at least one left?" Kevin asked.

The man shook his head. "No. Sorry."

"Is there some other place we might find one tonight?" Father asked him.

The man shook his head and gave their father an incredulous look. "Not a chance. It's late Christmas Eve with a heavy snow coming down." He turned to Corrie and Kevin, said "Sorry" again, and began walking to his truck.

"It's all right, Corrie," Kevin said, seeing her tears. "Father has another plan."

Corrie's tears quickly transformed to anger. "No he doesn't. Christmas is ruined. He hasn't found a cure for Mother and we don't have a Christmas tree." She slumped into the snow on her knees, tears freezing on her cheeks.

Father bent down and lifted her to her feet. He held her tight and whispered, "Corrie, we don't give up. We'll find a tree." His face was calm and peaceful. She looked into his eyes for a sign of hope that he could deliver on his promise.

"Sir," she heard then. The Christmas tree man had returned. "I hate to see these kids crying," he said. "In the back there are a few leftover trees. Nobody wanted them. You're welcome to one, no charge, if you can use it."

"Thank you. That's very kind," her father said.

Behind the barn a few pitiful trees were strewn about on the ground. They weren't much to look at. Corrie grabbed a bent tree.

"That's a fake tree," Kevin said. "I don't want a fake one."

"I think it's kind of pretty," Corrie said, trying to be optimistic.

Kevin grabbed a large one lying on its side. "How about this one?" But as he set it upright, most of the pine needles fell off. Now the artificial tree wasn't looking so bad.

"Did you hear that, Corrie?" Kevin asked.

"Hear what?"

"A voice! I heard a voice say, 'Pick me. I want to be your Christmas tree.'"

"You're crazy, Kevin. I think your brain has frozen. If you ever had one."

Kevin gave her a look that meant he'd like to punch her. Then he gasped. "I heard it again."

Corrie stared at him. "I did hear something, Kevin. I did!"

They stood quiet. Then came the faint words. "Pick me. I want to be your Christmas tree."

Corrie looked at her father to see if his lips were moving, but he had turned his head as if looking into the barn. Just then, there was a break in the clouds and the very brightest star in the sky seemed to be hovering right over the barn. Their father stood still but Corrie and Kevin went closer, very slowly.

Lying on its side, just inside the barn door beside some farm tools, was a little Christmas tree. Kevin touched the evergreen needles and they didn't fall off.

The base of the tree had a clump of dirt wrapped in a burlap bag. Corrie squealed with delight. "Daddy, come quick! Look." She pointed at the tree. "It's perfect. And it's alive. It's really alive."

Their father had a twinkle in his eyes. "I guess people thought it wasn't big enough to be a Christmas tree," he said.

"It's not too small," Corrie said. "And it can still grow. It's alive."

"It's your choice to make," Father said.

"Oh Daddy, how could we ever pick another tree after finding this one?"

Kevin laughed delightedly. "Father promised we would find a tree and we did."

Father bent down and picked up the little tree. His strong arms held it with great care. Driving back, Corrie thought the world was such a happy place with lights shining brightly all over town.

When they arrived home they went to show the tree to their mother and told her about the quiet voice they'd heard. She smiled through everything. The family tradition had been fulfilled.

They put the little tree on a small wooden table in a corner of the family room. They decorated it then sat for a while, just looking at the tree and drinking hot chocolate as the fire crackled in the fireplace. Their faces glowed from the lights on the tree and the warm flames.

Lying with their blankets on the rug between the Christmas tree and fireplace, Corrie and Kevin drifted off to sleep. Corrie knew when her father picked her up and tucked her into bed. The faint echoing words filled her wonderful dream and her heart. "Pick me. I want to be your Christmas tree."

The light of morning woke them. Corrie and Kevin ran into the family room.

"Merry Christmas, Corrie and Kevin," came a soft, familiar voice. That was Mother! They both whirled around. Corrie saw her mother looking like she wasn't in pain anymore.

"Mother!" Corrie said. "You're better."

Mother smiled and looked at the little Christmas tree. Tears came into her eyes. She seemed to be thinking of a faraway place, a better place, a place without pain. Then she said softly, "Children, my life has truly been blessed by you, with lots of happiness, loving friends, a wonderful husband, and a Savior born long ago on Christmas Day."

Father came into the room. Their mother smiled a peaceful contented smile at him. He took the family Bible from the mantle as the warmth of the fireplace filled the room and contentment filled their hearts. They settled in to hear him read the Christmas story found in Luke 2:8-20.

Corrie thought about the angels saying, "Don't be afraid," and "I bring you great joy." She thought about God picking shepherds to be the ones to find

Jesus in a manger in that stable.

Corrie looked at the little tree with its lights shining brightly. She looked at her mother who was well enough to come and sit in the rocking chair by the fire.

"I just realized something," she said. "We didn't pick our Christmas tree. It picked us. It was right there waiting for us to find it."

They all smiled. That was the best Christmas ever.

- David Knox Barker

The rest of the story…

Those who know my extended family may recognize much of this story.

It's difficult to come to terms with pain and suffering in its many forms, especially during the Christmas season. After all, Christ whose birth we celebrate is the Great Physician, with all power to heal in his hands. It is difficult to accept that how and when he chooses to heal is the work of Divine Providence, and that his eternal purpose is always at work in our lives.

If, during this Christmas season, like the family in this story, you can only accept Christ's gift of salvation, a gift that requires no gift in return, then you too can experience a perfect Christmas. A peace that carries pain and suffering beyond the limiting sphere of earth and into heaven itself is yours for the asking.

9

Angels in the Snow

As a child, I enjoyed making snow angels. I lay in a fresh blanket of snow, moving my arms and legs back and forth to make wings and the angel's skirt. Then I carefully got up so I wouldn't damage the powdered-sugar-like silhouette.

As an adult, "snow angels" were again part of my life. Although invisible to me, these gave visible help in seasons of need.

When our high-school-aged daughter considered attending Central Washington University, I drove her to Ellensburg to visit the college. It was my first drive over Snoqualmie Pass in the Cascade Mountains. We stayed on campus later than anticipated, and on our trip home, the unfamiliar route seemed dark and scary. Soon blinding snow began to fall, and I could barely see the lane lines and freeway's edge.

I prayed for safety as I crept along mile after mile, my knuckles white on the steering wheel. My daughter offered to drive, but she had no experience driving in snow, so I continued, hoping I wouldn't drive off the roadway or get stuck.

Suddenly, a light appeared ahead. Thinking it must be another car, I kept my focus on the light and followed it. I expected to catch up with the beam, but it always stayed just far enough ahead so I couldn't see what it was. I wondered if it was a snowplow, or my personal star of the East. Whatever it was, it guided me and gave me courage. We weren't alone in the snowstorm.

When we reached the summit, where road conditions improved, the light disappeared as quickly as it had appeared. I saw no car or snowplow or anything to account for the light. Perhaps a snow angel had shown me the way.

Years later, on a wintry day I headed out to get the mail. The new-fallen snow glistened in the sunshine, but it covered frozen puddles on our street. Unaware of the slippery surface beneath, I stepped on an icy patch and lost my footing. I expected to crash hard on my tailbone with a loud crack. But instead, my fall took place in slow motion. As my feet lifted from under me, it felt as if someone gently lowered me. I landed sitting in the soft snow, unharmed. I thanked God for his protection by my snow angel.

Another snowy day, my husband came home and told me about his experience as he traveled to work on the freeway. Cars ahead of him skidded out of control and blocked lanes. He couldn't stop and saw no way to avoid hitting them. Then his car wove in and out of the dangers as if navigated by someone else. He emerged on the other side and proceeded on course. Another snow angel?

Each of these experiences reminds me of God's promise in Psalm 91:11. *"He will give His angels charge concerning you, to guard you in all your ways."* (NASB) Although these incidents happened years ago, I will always remember God's love and protection when he sent guardian angels in the snow.

- Lydia E. Harris

10

Dreading Christmas

December seemed to be the steamroller month for my family. The weight of tragedies and grief piled upon, rolled over, and flattened our spirits. By 1989, we had come to the point of dreading December.

It all began in 1988, when my father died on December 7. His funeral was two days after my thirty-fifth birthday, and during my pregnancy with his only grandchild.

Two days after Dad's burial, my mother, who had been diagnosed with breast cancer before he had his fatal stroke, had no choice but to go ahead with a scheduled mastectomy. Adding to the grief in our household that Christmas, my mother-in-law was hospitalized, too.

December 1989 brought the death of my father-in-law. Because he died right before Christmas, his funeral was scheduled for the week after Christmas. I was concerned no one would attend except a few family members. In sad desperation, I called people I thought might take time from their seasonal activities to attend. Adding insult to injury, my calls resulted in not one additional attendee. Heaping another dilemma on the misery, our six-month-old son contracted the flu.

On December 7, 1993, my mother barely got seated in a car with friends from her community club when the car accelerated for some unknown reason, and didn't stop until it hit a brick column in a neighbor's yard. My mother, who hadn't had time to buckle her seat belt, took the brunt of impact. Because her injuries were internal, the emergency room staff did not see the extent of her injuries upon arrival. She almost bled to death. Again, our Christmas spirits got steamrolled.

We enjoyed a few reprieve Christmases, but the week of Christmas in 2004 my husband came down with the flu and did not feel up to attending our family Christmas dinner. We missed his presence, but my mother, brother, son and I had an enjoyable meal. Conscious of the preschool where I worked being a germ factory, I avoided hugging my mother goodbye since she suffered from a heart ailment and osteoporosis. My son told her goodbye, offering a gentle hug lest he damage her weakened bones.

The next day my brother called. He said mother was in the hospital and not expected to live through the night. I could hardly believe his words. She had seemed well the day before, despite her frailty.

I called our pastor's wife, Aggie, a nurse who wasn't working the day after Christmas. She drove me and my son to the hospital and stayed in mother's room with us. Because she had experience with dying patients, she kept us updated, moment-by-moment, which was a relief. Otherwise we would have been clueless.

Aggie directed us to hold mother's hands and speak with her. She prayed for our family and comforted us. Her care for us that evening became one of the sweetest Christmas gifts I have ever received. My mother went peacefully to be with Jesus while we remained by her side telling her we loved her.

A few days later however, it seemed the lights of Christmas season all switched to dim as my mother's friends from her small congregation gathered for the funeral and prepared to serve lunch afterwards. My husband, still sick with the flu and confined to bed, could not attend. My spirits momentarily lifted when I thought of my pastor and a church member who had driven over an hour to attend. Another close friend drove several hours to attend. Yet even with their support, I still felt alone without my husband by my side.

The time arrived for my brother, my son, and me to take our reserved seating. I sat down resigned to my bad attitude and feeling defeated by this newest loss at Christmas.

Looking at the casket surrounded by flowers, I was overwhelmed with regret that I had not hugged my mother after our Christmas family meal. Overcome with the weight of that guilt, I glanced to the side of my mother's casket, only to see a ceramic Nativity scene on display. Had someone forgotten that this was not a celebration of Christmas, but was my mother's funeral? I thought for a moment that someone had been disrespectful in their haste of setting up for the funeral.

But then it was as if I received a nudge from the Holy Spirit. "Look, really look."

My eyes focused upon baby Jesus in the manger. How peacefully he lay in his first bed beside my mother in her last bed.

My mother's body lay in her casket, but her soul had been transported to heaven where she was in the presence of Jesus. In God's timing I would get to see my mother alive again.

God gave me peace that passes understanding just like the Bible talks about. I received perfect closure on all the December tragedies and grief our family had suffered over the years.

I don't dread Christmas anymore, but welcome it.

Each Christmas, I thank the Divine Comforter who showed his presence at my time of need through a ceramic manger scene. Instead of being in misery over illness and death, I focus on a baby in a manger, who lived, died, and lived again so that I and my loved ones celebrate not just his birthday, but his presence with us and our eternal life.

~ Janice S. Garey

11

A Christmas Lesson

We'd recently moved from my childhood home in southern California to Missouri, which I considered in the middle of nowhere. Even though we'd lived on a farm in California, there was a huge culture shock moving halfway across the country to the Ozarks. In addition, I wasn't sure what the people were like.

It doesn't snow where I lived in southern California. In Missouri, the snow was over a foot deep as Christmas approached.

I'd left behind all my cousins, my horse, my friends at school and church. As an only child I'd never felt so alone in my life.

One night, about midnight, I woke up to hear my parents rushing through the house, shouting. I heard screams coming from outside – animal screams – and a frightening orange glow permeated the house through the windows. When I asked my father what was happening, he said, "The barn's on fire. We've got to get the animals out of there!"

Two sows had recently delivered babies, and we'd been keeping them warm in that barn. We were also keeping a young calf in there because of the extra cold temperatures.

We lived so far from town there was no fire department, so we were on our own. As Mom and Daddy ran out of the house, I was terrified. They wouldn't let me go outside. I stayed inside and watched through the window as my parents grabbed shovels and began to throw snow onto the barn, which was blazing far into the sky.

I decided this must be what hell was like as I listened to the screams of the terrified animals. Daddy had to put the sows out of their misery. He rescued the babies.

We were sure no one could get through to help us even if they'd known about the fire. However, I learned some things about Ozark country folks that night.

Someone had seen the flames. They'd called other neighbors, and to my amazement, they knew how to get through the snow. Some arrived in big pickup trucks, the beds loaded with bales of hay to weigh them down. Others drove their tractors. Through the front window I saw neighbors who lived two miles away riding in a trailer pulled by a huge John Deere tractor.

Within the hour, almost all of our country neighbors were shoveling snow to put the fire out. They kept it from spreading to our house and the other outbuildings – and they brought a feeling of warmth and community into my life that night that I've never forgotten.

Knowing we were surrounded by caring neighbors who helped replace farm equipment we'd lost made me feel a little less alone in this strange new world.

That was my eleventh Christmas. It was one I'll never forget.

- Hannah Alexander

❧ 12 ☙
The Red Birds

When Mama found out that she had terminal cancer, she did not think of herself, only her loved ones that she would have to leave behind. She vowed to make it one more Christmas with us because it was her favorite time of the year, celebrating the birth of her Savior and spending time with her family. She bought presents all year long and cooked a huge meal one last time since the doctors said she wouldn't make it to another Christmas.

She fooled them, though, and celebrated two more Christmases with us. On a New Year's Day she was taken to Hospice House in excruciating pain, her long journey of fighting the cancer rapidly coming to an end.

Daddy called to say the family needed to come and say our final good-byes. I left my children with my husband and drove to Hospice House. As I entered the room I saw Daddy standing beside Mama's bed along with her twin sister, Pat, my sister Pam, and brother Ricky. Three of my sisters' sons stood near the bed with tears in their eyes.

Except for low melodious sounds of Christmas music, all was quiet as we gathered around Mama's bedside.

The nurse came to check Mama's vitals. She smiled in a very tender way, the way she had probably smiled at many family members who were about to lose a loved one.

She put one hand on my daddy's shoulder. "It's almost time," she said. "I am so sorry, Mr. McKee."

My daddy looked tired, like he had aged about ten years in the past two, nursing Mama and waiting on her every minute of the day. He left her side only to go to the store or church. He said he didn't want to waste a moment they had left together.

Sorrow showed on his hollow face and then he did something I shall never forget. He began to sing along with the hymns playing on her CD player.

After a few surprised moments, one by one, we all joined him singing those gospel songs. As we sang the presence of the Holy Spirit became extremely strong in that hospital room.

Nurses gathered outside the door to listen to the family singing. One nurse remarked, with a hint of disbelief in her voice, "I have never heard a family sing so beautifully while their loved one is slipping away." The other nurses agreed that they, too, had never heard such beautiful singing.

We had prayed and asked God to bring healing to Mama's body if it would be his will. He chose to heal her in Heaven instead of here on Earth.

Mama left us a wonderful legacy of trusting God, even when we couldn't see his plan. She had never asked why this happened to her. Her praise had grown stronger as her body became weaker.

She loved Jesus and felt that she had run the race and finished the fight. She had made a profound positive impression during her illness with her upbeat attitude and peace in the midst of her storm. She said many times, "God has done more for me than I could ever deserve. Jesus shed his blood on the cross that I might have life eternally. I won't ask for another thing, but will offer praise and trust to the one who made me."

Pam shared with us that Mama had told her about a dream she had two months before the doctor diagnosed her cancer. In her dream, she had lain flat on her back in complete darkness. Then she looked up and saw who she knew was Jesus. Reaching her hand to him she pleaded, "Jesus, take my hand." Then she woke up from the dream.

Pam asked her son, who had brought his laptop along, to find the song with the words, "What a day that will be when my Jesus I shall see."

Soon, we were singing about what a day that would be, when Jesus we would see. He would take us by the hand and lead us to the Promised Land.

We sang along with that song over and over as if we were singing her into the arms of the angels who escorted her into heaven.

I'd always heard about a peace that passes all understanding. That day in Mama's room I experienced that peace first hand. I had thought we would all cry and be torn to pieces when Mama breathed her last breath. Instead, we sang. Knowing she had served God the best she could and was in heaven left us feeling comforted. The Holy Spirit came into the room with our family giving us a peace and strength that only He can give in our times of sorrow.

My son missed his grandmother so much he cried for her at least once a week for a long time. After about two years, he came to me one day crying about still missing her so much.

I told him I heard that when loved ones die they sometimes send a red bird to let you know they are all right and at peace. They want you to go on with your life and live it to the fullest.

After that, we began to see red birds at unexpected places and times. One night when I tucked him into bed, he said, "Mommy, Grandmother came to see me today at daycare. When I was on the playground I saw a red bird sitting on the fence watching me play and I knew she was there with me."

Tears filled my eyes and I kissed him on his forehead. "That's right, Joshua. She was making sure that you were having fun. You know how she loved to see little kids playing and being happy. She is happy too now knowing that you were playing with your friends and having fun."

He said his prayers and I pulled the covers up closer to him and told him goodnight. As I walked out of his room I was filled with amazement of how God cares so much about us that he would send a red bird to comfort a little boy who missed his grandmother.

I don't know that the story of the red bird is true or not. What I do know is that God is good. His love never fails and His mercies are new each morning.

We are reminded of that each Christmas by a little red bird tree ornament.

~ Kimberly Pickens

⧽ 13 ⧼

A Night Wrapped in Song

> Christmas Eve was a night of song that wrapped itself about you like a shawl.
> But it warmed more than your body. It warmed your heart...
> filled it, too, with a melody that would last forever.
>
> ~ Bess Streeter Aldrich

A chilly wind blew as I huddled with other carolers outside our country church. I breathed in the cold, crisp night air and shivered with excitement. After years of waiting, I could carol with the church choir. With church folk scattered throughout the rural area around Blaine, Washington, it would take all night to carol at each member's doorstep. Bundled in my green woolen scarf and new gloves, I couldn't wait to begin.

I remembered past Christmas Eves when I had watched my seven older brothers and sisters leave the warmth of our family gathering at 11 p.m. to carol. I had longed to go with them. As a young child, at bedtime I begged my mother, "Please, wake me when the carolers come." She always tried, but sometimes she couldn't rouse me.

As I grew older, my mother found it easier to awaken me in the middle of the night. Sleepy-eyed and pajama-clad, I would peek out the dormer window of our large green-and-white farmhouse. I listened dreamily to the carolers with my nose pressed against the frosty window. They sounded like angels, singing, "Joy to the World" and "Silent Night." I returned their cheerful shouts of "Merry Christmas!" and nestled back in bed, wishing I could have joined in the fun.

Now, after years of yearning and waiting, I was finally a teenager and my turn had come. A few snowflakes would make it perfect.

The choir director's voice interrupted my dreaming. "Let's get organized," he said. "How many of you can take your cars?" I looked around at the young men offering to drive. I hoped to sit in the front seat between a couple of them. But teenage girls experienced at flirting won those seats. I piled into the backseat with friends, just excited to be going along.

We laughed and chatted as we drove through the countryside, stopping to sing for church members. By starlight and flashlight, we crunch-crunch-crunched our way over the frozen ground to the front doors of farmers' homes. Most folks expected us and flung their doors wide open, inviting us in for a snack, even at two or three in the morning. Sipping hot chocolate by the crackling fires warmed us inside and out. Their generous hospitality led the choir director to limit the number of families allowed to feed us. Otherwise, we'd get sick from feasting in each home. Even so, we waddled to the cars stuffed like fat Christmas geese.

We continued our caroling refueled with Sloppy Joes, hot dogs, and fudge. As the night wore on, our throats wore out from singing in the winter air. We sounded more like croaking frogs than the angelic choir I remembered hearing as a child.

After arriving home at five in the morning, I snuggled beneath my thick handmade quilt. I tried to snatch a few hours of sleep before the Christmas morning church service where the choir would sing again. But it was hard to fall asleep with the excitement so fresh in my mind.

The night had been better than I imagined. No, I hadn't heard angelic hosts sing "Glory to God in the Highest" to country shepherds, but I had sung of His birth to country church members. I hadn't seen one bright star in the sky, but I had sung by starlight about that "star of wonder, star of night." I hadn't bowed at a manger to touch a newborn infant, but God had touched me as I worshiped the newborn King when I sang, "O come, let us adore Him."

More than forty years later, all-night caroling on Christmas Eve remains a treasured memory. I savor those magical nights wrapped in song that warmed me like my new woolen scarf.

~ Lydia E. Harris

The rest of the story…

A few years ago, I returned to the Mennonite church of my childhood and asked the pianist, "Does the choir still carol all night on Christmas Eve?"

Her face broke into a wide grin. "We sure do!"

On Christmas Eve in northwestern Washington, carolers will again awaken sleepy-eyed children and serenade waiting families. They'll stuff themselves with homemade treats throughout the frosty night. Little ones will long to join the caroling choir and sing praises to the Christ Child under starlit skies.

It cheers my heart to know the caroling tradition lives beyond my dreams, creating treasured memories for another generation of youthful carolers.

> *Sing to the Lord, for he has done glorious things;*
> *let this be known to all the world.*
> Isaiah 12:5 (NIV)

≈ 14 ≈
No Need to Fear Falling

Atop a ten foot ladder in my foyer, I located a string of burned-out Christmas lights – fixed those – and was hanging white and gold ornaments close to the top of the Christmas tree while worrying about falling.

I cautioned myself not to misstep. Besides no one being around to take me to the hospital if I fell, my mother's demise began when she fell off a chair and broke her leg while changing a light bulb.

Then the phone rang. Wondering who would call so late, I carefully descended the ladder and hurried to the kitchen for the phone. My daughter – a state away at college – was on the line. "Mom," she said. "The dealership repaired my car. But are you sitting down? You're not going to believe the bill."

I almost fell down when she told me the cost! Aghast at the four-figure amount, I replied, "I can't write a check to pay a bill like that. Have you called—"

"Yes," she said. "But no help's coming from that end. I was told to call you." She was obviously stressed. "Mom, how am I going to get home for Christmas?"

Pacing the floor, I became stressed. "What about your friends? Can you catch a ride home with one of them and we'll get the car issues straightened out after Christmas?"

"Everyone from home has already left campus and besides, the dealership wants me to pick up my car before they close tonight." She sounded as helpless as I felt. "They want their money. What can I do?"

Here it was Christmas and we were both crying or close to tears. Burned-out bulbs and bills were not what the holiday was supposed to be about. We should be joyful and celebrating the birth of our Lord instead of sad and fearful, worrying about how to pay for car repairs.

I thought about Dad. "Daddy!" I cried within my heart. "I so need to talk to you!" I didn't want to upset him with my problems. He would already be in bed anyway. He'd gone through recovery from having bladder cancer and now had prostate cancer. Also, having an enlarged heart that suffered an attack when Mom fell, he was not a well man. Borrowing money from him was out of the question.

Brought up to be independent, I felt that being a grown woman, it was my place to look after my parents and see to their needs – not the other way around. And my dad didn't need to know I was hurting. No parent should have to see a child in pain. I knew how that felt.

My credit card flashed through my mind, along with a headache. I hated charging anything and being in debt. But it seemed I had no other choice.

"Mom? Are you there?"

I choked back my fears while pulling out my confident voice. "I'm still here. Don't worry, honey. I'll call and give the dealership my credit card. I can't wait to have you home for Christmas." I rattled on about positive things. "We're going to have fun making Red Velvet cake. I'm trimming the tree now. Tomorrow night, let me know when you're thirty minutes out and I'll have hot chocolate simmering."

"Thanks, Mom." She sounded much relieved. "Love you."

After giving the dealership my credit card number and hanging up the phone, the blood-rushing-to-my-head feeling worsened along with the pounding. Continuing to pace the floor, thinking of the payments I'd have to make, I envisioned grooves forming in the hardwood beneath my feet.

Finally, I did a last-resort kind of thing. I cried out to heaven and poured out a bucket load of sorrows. Within a few minutes, I felt a total peace wash over me. Calm. The noise in my head – gone. Stillness and quiet flowed in. I knew this would work out…somehow.

The Christmas tree beckoned from the foyer for a few last-minute touches. No fear of falling now. As I topped the tree with an angel who would be keeping watch, the phone rang again. My heart felt heavy. Worry returned. Who could be calling this late? Don't tell me. A flat tire? Please God. No more bad news. "Let it be someone else with no problems," I pleaded aloud. "A wrong number would be great!"

"Vicki?" The sleepy sounding voice was Daddy's. The knots in my stomach tightened as my knuckles whitened. Where had my calm and peace gone? "Are you all right?" he asked.

"Yes." I quickly let out my breath. "Are you all right? What are you doing up this late? You should have been asleep an hour ago."

"I was asleep. But woke up because I heard you crying out like you were in distress. You sure you're okay?"

How had he heard me crying out?

"Vicki, you sounded like you were in deep trouble."

Could it be that while in anguish and desperately calling out my daddy's name that God had allowed him to supernaturally hear me? It had to be. There was no other explanation. This was too good to keep to myself. And Daddy needed to know he wasn't dreaming or going crazy. He really did hear me calling him.

Through joyful tears, I explained the night's dilemma. Without hesitation Daddy said, "All you have to do is drive to my house and write yourself a check. We have to get that child home for Christmas."

"Daddy, I don't want you worrying. The problem has already been taken care of and I'm okay with my decision. The reason I'm telling you about it now is because God's watching over us is too good to keep to myself. My heavenly Father heard me and contacted my earthly father because he knew I needed to talk with you. I think he wanted your child and your grandchild to know you're our earthly backup if we need one." I felt that incredible peace and joy. "Isn't that amazing God would wake you by allowing you to supernaturally hear my cry of desperation?"

"Yeah," Daddy said, wide awake now. "That's amazing alright. But next time, instead of pacing the floor until you make yourself sick, call me, little girl."

After hanging up the phone, I walked down the hall and stopped to admire my creativity. The angel was still where I'd placed her atop the tree. After the night's happenings, I wouldn't have been surprised if she'd given me a wink and a smile and jumped off the tree to dance. She didn't.

I turned out the foyer light before retiring to bed. But somewhere close by, I knew my guardian angel was twirling a time or two and grinning like a

Cheshire cat with a stash of Christmas catnip.

Lying in bed, I marveled about the incident that for a few minutes had turned my world upside down. The outcome wasn't what I'd anticipated. God's plan was to let me know he was listening, and he made sure my deepest prayer was answered by connecting my earthly father to my needs.

The subject of possible future problems popped into my mind. Car problems were especially dreadful. But if I didn't have problems, there would be no need for God to show himself by using other people, therefore no amazing stories to share with unbelievers as well as believers.

Glad my present ordeal was over, I knew I wouldn't trade my experience since I survived it; but I sure dreaded the next moment of chaos, because Jesus said, "In this world you will have troubles."

Yet I also knew that God meant it when he said, "Don't worry about anything but pray about everything. Tell God what you need, and thank him for all he has done. Then you will experience God's peace, which exceeds anything we can understand. His peace will guard your hearts and minds as you live in Christ Jesus."

Like Dorothy's mantra in the *Wizard of Oz*, "There's no place like home," I repeated my own mantra, "There's no need to fear falling."

Then I reached over and turned out the lamp light, knowing the real light would never burn out but always be shining, and one day bulb replacement would be a thing of the past.

"Merry Christmas to all and to all a good night," I whispered.

~Vicki H. Moss

ꙮ 15 ꙮ
SNOWFLAKE PARTY

It's 1998 and the first snow of winter hasn't fallen yet, but in our kitchen tonight we're doing a pretty good imitation. The whole family is circled around the huge old oak table. The snip, snip, snip of scissors is background music for giggles and good-natured ribbing, and exclamations of "Oh, wow! Look at that one!" Tiny scraps of white paper float down from the table, making our floor look like a giant brownie sprinkled with powdered sugar.

Tonight has turned out to be the night for our annual Snowflake Party. The tradition began when our children were just toddlers. There has never been a date blocked out in red on our calendar, but nevertheless, a year rarely goes by that we don't celebrate the event.

It's one of those things that just happens. One day we wake up and the brisk autumn air has turned bitter. Naked tree branches trace their stark calligraphy on a dull grey sky. It's that time of limbo between the crisp anticipation of autumn's new beginnings and winter's joyful promises of Christmas and snow. The perfect time for a party.

On such a day, one of the kids will fly in the back door, fresh home from school, and say, "Hey, Mom! Tonight would be a good night for the Snowflake Party!"

First we have to round up every pair of scissors in the house. This is one time when sharing is not a virtue. While the kids search for scissors, I scavenge every piece of plain white paper I can get my hands on. When I've collected at least five or six sheets for each member of the family, the pieces are cut into squares and folded catty-corner multiple times. The resulting triangles are artfully arranged in a basket, awaiting the beginning of the party.

Later, when supper dishes are drying on the counter, and all the crumbs and jelly spots have been wiped from the tabletop, I recruit a volunteer to help me stir up a big pot of hot cocoa. It will mull and warm on the back burner, tantalizing us with its aroma for the next hour.

Now the fun begins. Everyone claims a pair of scissors...no fighting allowed. Then begins the careful cutting and snipping, shaping plain white paper into intricate works of art. Each snowflake we create seems as unique and spectacular as the genuine variety created by God himself.

As each masterpiece is unfolded, collective oohs and aahs go up. Now the iron is pressed into duty, smoothing the creases and folds from each delicate creation. A spritz of starch is the finishing touch.

When the last dregs of our creative juices are drained, Dad oversees the vacuum patrol while I pour warm cocoa into generous mugs. We spread our handiwork on the floor all around us and sit, quietly admiring our work while we dunk marshmallows and sip rich chocolate.

Later, with empty mugs piled up in the sink, it's time for the judging to begin. There will be awards for cutest, prettiest, most unusual, most like the real thing, and as many other categories as we need for everyone to be a winner. Dad is the judge because he studied art in college. He also usually wins one of the top prizes – because he studied art in college.

Snowflakes deemed runners-up might be pasted in scrapbooks or hung on the refrigerator. A few even "melt" into the trash that very night. But the winners are taped proudly to the big picture windows in the living room for passersby to enjoy while they long for the day when genuine snowflakes will color the world clean and white.

Our oldest daughter went far away to college last September. She called just after Thanksgiving to tell me that her dorm window was covered with snowflakes. No, not the real thing, but the ones she remembers from her childhood – paper ones that she spent an entire evening cutting and snipping while sipping hot cocoa.

That's the neat thing about traditions: They go with us no matter how far from home we might travel.

- Deborah Raney

≈ 16 ≈
Noel, the Cat Who Came for Christmas

I dreaded the prospect of aging. Yet, the inevitable had come like taxes and morning breath. Gazing into the mirror, I concluded I could no longer hold to the illusions of eternal youth. But, how does one gracefully glide into the night while still worshipping the day? I looked for someone to teach me and found a hero in my cat.

We already owned two male cats and hadn't wanted more. Yet, there she was, an adult cat sitting on our porch, licking her fur, and acting like the princess of 900 Greene Street. She knew she had found a home before we even knew she needed one.

It was nearing Christmas and a familiar scripture came to memory, pulling at my senses like a nagging child: *I tell you the truth, whatever you did not do for one of the least of these, you did not do for me.* (Matthew 25:45)

But, like the Levite in the Good Samaritan story, we passed by while she huddled in a cold corner of the porch.

When she clung to her post, I felt remorse, as if she'd been sent to us. After three days, I could stand the guilt no longer. We brought her in and named her Noel in honor of the season.

At first, Noel roamed while we slept and became invisible during the day, occasionally allowing us a glimpse of her brown, tiger-striped body as she scurried up the stairs to hide. She remained secluded, refusing to eat while the home's inhabitants were active.

Soon, her fear gave way to curiosity. She sauntered into the living room to examine us, yet remained aloof. The slightest attempt at affection sent her flying back up the steps to her secret place.

This sleuthing continued for the next six months until the day she decided to engage us. I was reading a book and sipping a freshly brewed cup of coffee when I became aware of loud purring and an inexplicable weight on my tummy. Distracted from my comfort, I found Noel resting on my lap. Then she started nipping at my hand.

I thought about ignoring her just as she had ignored us. Tenacious to the core, she continued nipping until I had no choice but to stop reading and either pet her or push her off my lap. I chose the first option, and the purring resumed. It was the beginning of a long and great friendship.

As my children left home one by one, Noel's tenacity continued to characterize her disposition into old age. Despite her hefty bulk and arthritic joints, she fought for first sitting rights. Even to the last, she battled with our two male cats for lap supremacy, the younger felines scooting for safety whenever Noel hissed.

Noel braved whatever life threw her way, including the ravages of age.

Already grown when she found us, she stayed for twenty years.

Among the many things she taught us was that life is precious at any age. With her help, I learned that age cannot altar my spirit, for that belongs to God. Though the flesh withers, God will sustain me until he calls me home.

I am grateful that God sent her to us, teaching me how she withstood pain with the same fierce determination she had when she first decided to grace us with her love on that blustery Christmas day.

Even to your old age and gray hairs, I am he,
I am he who will sustain you.
Isaiah 46:4a

~ *Linda Wood Rondeau*

17

The Amazing Gift

Brenda adjusted the red silk pillows before she sat on the teak bench. She took a deep breath and said, "The candle you're burning smells scrumptious — like vanilla cupcakes."

I nodded. "It's Buttercream. I like it better than the Mistletoe and Holly we usually light this time of year."

She looked around. "There's something special about this place. I felt it the minute I walked in."

"Thanks," I said, and smiled at the thought. That's what all my customers say about my Serenity Spa.

I liked the way the sunlight glinted on garlands of evergreen on each window and filled the entry of the small spa with a warm glow. But that's not what made it special. After several years of owning the salon, I realized my success or failure had little to do with my business savvy, or talent regarding hair and skin care. This place was unique because relationships formed here. We talked about God's presence here. His light made it sparkle like a gem in this quaint Florida town – especially at Christmastime.

Special friendships formed here. Brenda's presence was proof of that. Her friend had said, "Brenda needs to have her hair styled before my Christmas party and will stop by. You just have to hear her story."

Now I sat next to her as she took a sip of the green tea I served, then she began. "A frigid rain fell that day in December. I woke up with a terrible cough. A few days later I went to the doctor, who sent me to a pulmonary specialist. My appointment was in January. I was put on oxygen. That meant I couldn't participate in a church outreach retreat in which I was to help in the kitchen, because there were two huge gas stoves in that kitchen."

Her smile began to fade. "I knew if my life had really deteriorated to the point where I couldn't give of myself, or work, or even enjoy my family and friends – I needed help. That's when I knew I needed a miracle."

A miracle.

I looked down at my cup. Felt the silence. Then I looked at her again and thought she was waiting for my question. I asked, "What happened next?"

She smiled. "Well, I just kept praying. And finally…I asked the Lord to heal me. I figured, God always provided for me through all my heartaches of lost love and other hardships I'd been through, so I started concentrating on being thankful for everything – the good and the bad – that would bring me closer to him."

Brenda's voice rang with such sincere warmth as she told her story. "The miracle is my change of attitude. God had helped me through many trials and storms. I began to look at this as an opportunity to become a better person. His peace replaced my fear. It was up to him if I'd ever be able to breathe on my own again – if I lived or died."

She talked about being on the list for a lung transplant and then receiving the surgery a few months ago. "I developed some severe setbacks during my recovery. I clung to a special verse of scripture that helped me through my darkest hours. I believe the Lord brought me through the surgery to help others keep a positive attitude in times of illness or sorrow. As long as I have breath, I want to tell people about God's amazing gift of love. So, every step I took toward recovery, no matter how hard, was a step toward proving God is my provider, my rock – my Christmas miracle."

I tried to say something – anything – without crying. All I could manage was a whisper. "What verse is it?"

"Jeremiah 29:11."

I longed to get my Bible and find the verse but the subject turned to hair. Later, looking lovely with her new style, Brenda hugged me and began to recite the verse. "I know the plans I have for you, declares the Lord…" she started.

I repeated the rest of the verse after her. "Plans to give you hope and a future."

She smiled and hugged me tighter, then stepped away. "Goodbye Joann. I suspect God placed you here at Serenity Spa for more reasons than you know. He is using you in mighty ways. I'm glad you let me tell you about my journey." She advised, "Never let go of the true wonder of Christmas, Joann, the birth of a child who died to offer us forgiveness."

Forgiveness.

After she left, I thought about Brenda's walk with God. As she was telling her story, we both seemed to know it wasn't only about her being a medical miracle – or the fact that she needed a new hairstyle. No one had told her about the pain I hid inside. I knew that without a doubt, because I had told no one. There was a reason we met and she shared her story.

In those quiet moments alone, God's presence filled my heart and stirred my soul.

"You know the reason, my child…"

Two years had passed since my sister and I had spoken to each other.

I had missed my niece's wedding. There had been no crazy-loud Thanksgiving family gathering this year, or last.

I couldn't forget the crime her son committed. It tore at my heart and kept me up at night. I couldn't sing. I wouldn't write. I wanted to erase all the time I had spent praying for him when he was a child. I wished to blot out his name and any memory of the teen he had become.

"If anyone could forgive him, surely it would be you, Joann," my sister had pleaded. And then she accused, "You're supposed to be a Christian!"

She could not have hurt me more if she'd slapped me. I'd rather she had.

I needed to strike back. "None of us will ever be the same because of his actions," I said, but really meant, I will never be the same. She and I could no longer communicate. How could I forgive her? Or her son?

And so I carried that heavy burden and hid it away in my heart. For several months I had read everything I could about forgiveness. I went to the salon every day, and cried out to God every night. When my family slept, my spirit woke me – like clockwork, at 3:00 a.m. I had a long list of whys? Why don't I understand your ways, Lord? Why didn't I see this storm coming? I tried to lead him…to you. Why did I believe his lie? And why did you let me?

Now, almost two years later, I sat alone in the salon, the early afternoon sunlight shaded behind a huge live oak. I went into the facial room and shut the door. I got down on my knees and cried out to God once more. "Please hear my prayer, Lord. I hide behind the stories I try to write and the songs I try to sing. I'm inhibited, not free. I think my childlike spirit died when he —. Why?"

I remembered Brenda saying she changed her attitude. I returned to my prayer. "Okay, Lord. The only Why I'm asking now is, why did you lead Brenda here? I'm ready to move on. Christmas is right around the corner. I'm certain you sent Brenda here today, and I'm thankful you've led so many broken souls to this salon. You created a haven to reveal your heart to them, and always, to me. I may not understand or agree how you work, but I do want to forgive —. "

Forgive? My child, forgiveness is not a word. It is an action. And like my grace, it is a gift. Perhaps you can give this same gift to others, as I have given it to you.

My heart answered, "Father, I miss my sister. I want to forgive like you did the day your son gave his life for me. I don't want my story to end this way. Thank you for leading Brenda here today. She's gone through so much and yet she accepted the good, and the bad as gifts. Help me become more like her. More like you."

I went home and called my sister. I told her Brenda's story. I asked her forgiveness. We both cried. Then we laughed. A week later we joined our families for a Christmas gathering like we'd had many times in the past. I snapped a picture of my niece and her adoring husband on the couch, cuddling their one-year-old daughter. I took a few pictures of my nephew – the one God used in my life to teach me about forgiveness.

My favorite picture is one of my sister and me sitting by the Christmas tree, smiling, surrounded by a room full of gifts.

Every day, we have opportunities for God to prove his love for us, if we ask, if we believe. The Father's gifts can come in all kinds of packages. Some are beautiful. Some are broken. All of them wrapped in stories worth telling.

Many of them…Christmas miracles.

All of them, amazing gifts.

~ Joann M. Claypoole

18

The Christmas Babies

Tears streamed down my face as my son knelt, then lay prostrate in front of the church altar, giving his life to the Lord. The years fell away as I thought back to the birth of my Christmas baby.

The labor room clock read 11:45 p.m. and the doctor said, "Ok, Julie, push. Let's have this baby on Christmas Eve." Being overdue, I really didn't care when the baby came; I just wanted it over with. I did all I could, but he didn't appear until 12:15 Christmas morning, 1972.

Grinning from ear to ear, the doctor said, "Wow, nine and one-half pounds! What a Christmas present!"

Our older son, just two years of age, kept saying, "Jesus," as he pointed at the bundle in my arms.

"No, sweetie, he was born on Jesus' birthday, but he's not Jesus." My husband and I both assured him, "He's your little brother, Ryan."

Now, forty-two years later, I marveled at Ryan being ordained into the ministry after finally answering God's call. No, he wasn't Jesus, but this man, born on Christmas day, was publicly stating he was ready to go out into the world to share the good news about a miraculous gift from God, Jesus, the real Christmas baby.

~ *Julie Hale Maschhoff*

Afraid of Christmas

As Christmas approached I became increasingly afraid. Being a single mom, I couldn't imagine recreating for my girls the kind of special memories I had of Christmases with Mom, Dad, and my brother.

My first Christmas as a single mom was hardest. There was no dad to take toys from hard molded plastic packaging, read directions, find a screwdriver and put together toys in a way that seemed impossible for me. No dad taking pictures of them laughing and smiling and tearing away the paper from wrapped gifts, eager to find the surprise inside. No dad to hear their squeals of excitement.

Oh, how I agonized over every plan for that special day. I lay in bed at night, asking how in the world I was ever going to make them happy and create memories like I had as a child.

I scrimped and saved to make their Christmas special. I bought the tree and decorated it with bright lights, sparkling and colorful ornaments. Like my mom had done years before in our home, I placed homemade decorations throughout the apartment. I wrapped the boxes, filled with new clothes, in colorful paper with curly bows and lay them beneath the tree. Memories from my childhood were taking shape for my young children to enjoy.

The girls and I baked cookies together a few days before Christmas. The older one helped decorate by sprinkling colored sugar on the cookies after I cut them out. We made sure to have some decorated sugar cookies ready to lay out for Santa. I baked banana bread and blueberry muffins. Ingredients were mixed and ready to be turned into hot chocolate on Christmas morning. I had done the best I could to give the girls my memories.

I decided to start a new tradition for our family and let them open one gift, that I guided them to, on Christmas Eve. They loved opening the gifts and getting their new pajamas.

As I read *The Night Before Christmas* to them, my heart was breaking. My young children were being cheated out of the Christmas they should be having. With tears in my broken heart, I tucked them into bed. I sat on the couch and prayed for strength to make it through Christmas.

Later that night, I ate the cookies and drank the milk laid out for Santa, all the time thinking their dad should be doing it. I took the toys out of their hiding place and laid them under the tree, then filled their stockings with Santa goodies. After crying, while feeling sorry for myself and my children, I went to bed.

After my alarm went off at six on Christmas morning, I watched them hurry to see what Santa had left for them. Happy laughter sounded as they examined every toy, opened every package. They carefully examined all the little goodies in their stockings.

During the morning they had their fill of banana bread and hot cocoa and played with every toy. They didn't mind taking a nap in their new pajamas and holding their favorite toy before we headed to my parents' home for a Christmas dinner, grandparent gifts, and more goodies.

All had gone smoothly; only my broken heart knew they were not having a normal Christmas.

Thirty-five years later, my children are grown, married, and have children of their own. They started making their own traditions with their husbands.

At a gathering we began to talk about Christmas memories. During one of those discussions I learned the most astounding thing. My daughters thought they had normal Christmases.

My memory of their Christmases was not theirs. They did not remember their dad ever being there for Christmas because they were so young when he left. To them, our Christmases were normal. They hadn't had their hearts broken like I thought they were going to because the memories weren't there for them to compare.

Because of my preconceived idea of normal, I had worried in vain for years. That day I learned not to be afraid. What I create for my family is our normal.

As I remember those past Christmases, I know God was in control and gave my children their own special memories.

We don't need to recreate someone else's normal, not even our own childhood memories.

~ Lillian Humphries

20

The Christmas Blanket

The angel said unto them, "Fear not: for, behold, I bring you good tidings of great joy, which shall be to all people. For unto you is born this day in the city of David a Saviour, which is Christ the Lord."

Luke 2:10–11

My husband called from Afghanistan to let me know that, once again, he would not be coming home for Christmas. Then, almost as an afterthought, he shared that he had narrowly missed a bomb that morning. It had exploded less than a mile from him, killing four and wounding fifteen.

As a contractor in the Middle East, Rodney is always confronted with the threat of bullets, missiles and bombs. And as his wife, I'm always confronted with the fear associated with those threats of what could happen to my husband.

Of course, I was continually lifting Rodney up in prayer, but that didn't stop me from worrying about his safety.

But in the past year I had learned to pray differently. All because of what had happened the previous Christmas.

My three daughters and I had joined my mother and my sister for a Christmas Eve service at a nearby chapel located in our North Carolina mountains. The humble decorations of pine boughs and poinsettias and the candlelight that bounced off the mica in the stone walls set the mood. The chapel filled quickly as we found a pew and slid into our seats. As the pipe organ played softly, I glanced through the program and saw the expected traditional Christmas Eve service planned: Bible readings from the Gospel of Luke, singing of old familiar Christmas carols heralding the birth of Jesus Christ, and the lighting of the last candle of the Advent wreath.

What I didn't expect was the method in which the pastor started his Christmas Eve message titled "Fear Not." A projection screen was lowered as he set up a clip we were about to see from the animated television show, *A Charlie Brown Christmas*. He explained how Charlie Brown had become discouraged and depressed because he felt Christmas had become commercialized and trivialized. After receiving massive ridicule for choosing a sad tree for the Christmas play, a frustrated Charlie Brown begged for the answer to the question, "Isn't there anyone who knows what Christmas is all about?"

The clip began to play and we watched as Linus took the stage to explain to all the meaning of Christmas. Linus quoted Luke 2:8–14: *And there were in the same country shepherds abiding in the field, keeping watch over their flock by night. And, lo, the angel of the Lord came upon them, and the glory of the Lord shone round about them: and they were sore afraid. And the angel said unto them, "Fear not…"*

The preacher allowed the clip to continue until Linus completed verse 14 and exited the stage. The lights went up as well as the screen, and the preacher asked us to go home and watch the scene again, looking for something very specific. He asked us to pay close attention to the moment when the angels in scripture say, "Fear not!" At that moment Linus dropped his security blanket and boldly, passionately, shared the Good News. But once the message had been given and received, Linus picked up his blanket and exited the stage.

The preacher asked us to consider if we were like Linus – dropping our security blanket while focusing solely on God and what He is saying to us, only to pick up our blanket after our conversation with Him has ended.

I realized I was just like Linus, but instead of dragging around a security blanket, I was shrouding myself in a blanket of fear.

For years, I had dragged my fears with me everywhere: The fear of What Now? after Rodney lost his job before going to Afghanistan. Fear of having no money or constant source of income. Fear as financial devastation came crashing all around us. Fears of foreclosure on our home, major health issues, no health insurance, lack of food in the pantry and on the table. Fear of losing loved ones due to mental illness, substance abuse or bullets. The list went on and on.

As a Christian, I would confidently take these fears before God and lay them at the altar. Each time God would reassure me to "fear not." But as habit would have it, after sharing my heart and laying everything before Him, I would rise, pick up those fears and drag them off behind me.

So that Christmas Eve I went home and did what the preacher had asked of us. I watched the clip of Linus, on stage bolding proclaiming the Good News of the birth of our Savior. And I watched how the blanket fell from his hands. But I also watched the clip until the end of the special. Yes, Linus dragged the blanket off-stage with him after completing his soliloquy, but if you watch until the end of this Christmas special, Linus eventually takes his blanket and wraps it around the base of Charlie Brown's sad Christmas tree. Linus' blanket gave support to the tree, only then allowing the gang to decorate it, making something sad and withered into something beautiful.

As the gang began to sing the familiar carol, "Hark the Herald Angels Sing," I realized there was another blanket associated with Christmas that I had not considered before. On the holiest of nights, the baby Jesus had also been wrapped in a blanket. But he had been wrapped in a blanket, or swaddling clothes, for protection and for security. He was wrapped in a blanket that would give comfort and warmth. He was not given a blanket to carry through life to drag behind. This blanket was used the way it was intended on that blessed night and for all nights to come.

This past Christmas Eve I decided I would stop wrapping myself in blankets of fear or carrying them with me. Instead, I would bring my concerns before the altar and pray for my husband, leaving the missiles and bombs and bullets at God's feet. I decided I would not exit the stage having ignored God's word, carrying or dragging my blankets behind me.

Once again for Christmas, my husband will be on the other side of the world, away from his family, in one of the most dangerous places imaginable. I will miss him terribly; but Rodney and his safety have been laid at the altar.

So this Christmas I'll pop a bag of popcorn, curl up on the couch and watch *It's a Wonderful Life*. And I'll throw a blanket across my lap to keep me warm.

~ *Lori Marett*

21

The Fruitcake Caper

Fruitcake. You either love it or hate it. In our large family with eight children, everyone loved it.

But it wasn't just any fruitcake we wanted. We didn't crave the heavily brandied cakes in fancy tins or those without much candied fruit. We longed for Mother's homemade recipe – spicy, fruity, and with the crunch of walnuts. As it was cut, each slice revealed shiny jewels of colored citron, begging to be nibbled.

According to tradition, our family baked fruitcake around Thanksgiving and let it age until Christmas. I helped Mother measure the ingredients and mix the cake in her large aluminum bread bowl. We made several loaves and decorated the tops with candied cherries and halves of walnuts we had shelled.

As the fruitcake baked, the sweet, spicy aroma wafted through the house, and my mouth watered. After it was baked, we were allowed only a small taste before Mother stored the fruitcake in a large pressure cooker in the pantry to safely age until Christmas.

But one December, when Mother opened the pressure cooker on Christmas Day, she found a knife and only part of a fruitcake.

My oldest brother had been making secret stops by the pantry each morning to cut slices to add in his lunch box.

We didn't hold it against him…long. After all, it was the season of goodwill toward men, including brothers. Instead, we laughed that he got away with his fruitcake caper.

Many years have passed since then, but I often bake fruitcake at Thanksgiving, using Mother's prized recipe. My daughter and grandson help mix the batter in the old, now dented, aluminum bowl.

Sometimes I even mail a small loaf and a plastic knife to my brother, now in his eighties, and chuckle as I reminisce about his youthful fruitcake caper.

– Lydia E. Harris

Our Family's Fruitcake Recipe

In a medium saucepan combine and simmer until most of the water is absorbed:
- 1 pound raisins
- 2 cups water

Add and mix until shortening is melted:
- ²/3 cup shortening
- 1½ cups sugar

Stir in:
- 3 eggs, slightly beaten
- 1 teaspoon vanilla

Sift together:
- 3 cups flour
- 1 teaspoon salt
- 1½ teaspoons soda
- 1 teaspoon cinnamon
- ½ teaspoon cloves
- ¼ teaspoon nutmeg

Add the flour mixture to the raisin mixture alternately with
- 1 cup buttermilk.

Mix in thoroughly:
- 1 pound candied citron (or candied pineapple and cherries)
- 8 ounces candied cherries
- 1 cup chopped walnuts or pecans

Pour into two greased and floured loaf pans, or make some into mini-loaves or cupcakes. Decorate tops with cherries and nuts.

Bake at 325 degrees for approximately one hour. Test with toothpick for doneness.

Cool 15 minutes. Remove cake from pans. Cool completely.

Wrap in foil and store in the refrigerator.

Yield: 2 loaves. (I make some into mini-loaves or cupcakes to share with others.)

22

What I Didn't Want for Christmas

The story of Lazarus rising from the dead is a personal favorite. After all, what's not to love? Mary and Martha stand in the gap for their brother and Jesus delivers him from death as the world watches.

Then Jesus shouted, "Lazarus, come out!" And the dead man came out, his hands and feet bound in grave clothes, his face wrapped in a head cloth. Jesus told them, "Unwrap him and let him go!" (John 11:43–44 NLT)

This miraculous scene – which has brought me immeasurable hope in years past – has brought more questions than answers in years present. For longer than I care to admit, I lived in the shadow of silence while mental illness gnawed away at my brother's life. As time passed, he became even more depressed and still; Jesus was a no show. Mary, Martha, and me – all panicking and praying our guts out.

For three years I fasted, prayed, worshiped, wept, and slept with my Bible clutched against my chest. But, as my heart-cries grew more fervent, God seemed all the more quiet. No healing. No miracle. Instead of getting better, Jay slipped further away, like a song that ends with a slow fade. Our family tried everything to save him, yet his mental condition continued to rob my brother of dignity and strip his soul bare.

And then, just when I thought things couldn't get any worse, heaven's silence was deafening.

In December of 2011, I got the one thing for Christmas that I never, ever wanted.

"Penny. Penny! *Penny!*" My sister sobbed out my name over the phone.

That weekend, we both had tried to contact Jay. When our attempts proved unsuccessful and concern increased, she drove to his house. I listened to what she was trying to tell me on the phone, but refused to hear the tragic truth.

Our younger brother had barricaded himself in his bedroom and ended his pain the only way he knew how. It was never supposed to end like that.

I won't pretend to understand about Jay's suicide, but this I know. Although Jesus did not come in the manner I wanted him to that Christmas, he came.

Jesus came in my husband who held me as I wept.

Jesus came in the candle left on the porch by a stranger.

Jesus came in the makeshift memorial – a tribute of all things Jay.

Jesus came in the red and green wreath, hung amidst our mourning drab.

Jesus came in the compassion of friends.

Jesus came in the sunlight when darkness was all around.

Jesus came in the flowers sent from near and far.

Jesus came in the smudgy sentiments of little hearts laid bare.

And, Jesus came in the Christmas candlelight, soft and glowing.

While I find myself living out what looks like just another tragic drama, deep in the recesses of my shattered soul I must continue to hold onto the hope of Christmas. And, although I may not like the way this particular scene has played out, I must remember I am in the midst of a greater story whose triumphant end I know.

"I know that my Redeemer lives, and that in the end he will stand upon the earth." (Job 19:25 NIV)

Caskets aren't supposed to come at Christmastime. But when they do, Christ comes with them. I've learned that the pain I bear when death doesn't rise is actually God's gateway to the rising of new life in me.

"I tell you the truth, unless a kernel of wheat is planted in the soil and dies, it remains alone. But its death will produce many new kernels" – a plentiful harvest of new lives. (John 12:24 NLT)

Jesus came in the Christmas of 2011, and he will come again every Christmas…until he comes to take me home.

~ Penny A. Bragg

23

The Miracle Tree

Funny how what may seem like a fiasco can become the stuff of family traditions. The year of the miracle Christmas tree was one of those disasters that ultimately brought about a cherished tradition that would span generations in our family.

That year, our friends started their You-Pick Christmas Tree enterprise, opening their one-hundred acre homestead to Christmas tree seekers. Kerry, a physical therapist, and his wife, Rena, a nurse, offered to chop down any tree on their property for a mere five dollars. At that time, a live tree from the store cost anywhere from twenty-five to fifty dollars.

"Sounds like a good deal," I told my husband Steve. "All we have to do is show up. We don't even need to bring a saw. Plus, we get to spend an afternoon with Kerry and Rena. Piece of cake."

Life is rarely that simple. How were we to know the events that would follow?

I called Kerry and set a date to go tree hunting in his woods. When the day arrived, temperatures sank into single digits, and my determination waffled. However, sucking in courage, our family of five piled into our station wagon and headed for what I assured them would be a wonderful adventure.

Kerry led the way into the woods then pointed up at the towering pines. "Don't worry how high the tree is. Once it's cut down, we'll trim from the top."

We traipsed the woods for over an hour, and yet, not one tree beckoned me. About to give up, I turned my head to the right. The fullest tree I'd ever seen stood before me. "That's the tree I want!"

I would have jumped for joy if three feet of snow hadn't pinned me down.

I suppose any other man would have simply agreed to end the trek and get back to someplace warm. Not Steve. He knew me too well. Knew my visual assessments could be askew when shivering with cold. "Are you absolutely sure?" he asked.

"As sure as when we got married."

Steve's objections silenced, Kerry chopped the tree down, shortening it at the spot I thought would work. Eying its long green needles, I imagined how beautiful it would look in just a few days.

Our children, ages nine, ten, and eleven, laughed as they pointed at its challenging length. Steve, well aware of my inability to sight-measure, clucked with worry. "I doubt I can even get it on top of the car." When my eyes filled with tears, he gave my hand a reassuring squeeze. "We'll figure something out."

Half an hour later, exhausted from the haul back to the house, Steve dropped the tree by the parked station wagon. Our daughter Edie, as if confronting a monster, gazed in wonder at the Goliath prostrate on the ground. "Even if we make it home, we won't be able to get it into the house," she prophesied.

Perhaps a part of me had already regretted my impulsiveness. Looking for a glimmer of hope, I found comfort in my husband's solidarity. He eyed the tree then pointed at our daughter. "You just let me worry about that." Using every bungee cord in his toolbox, he secured the tree and ordered us into the car.

I glanced at my prize, and now that I was sans rose-colored glasses, I slunk into the passenger seat. Doubt quickly eroded my joy. Too late now. We'd have to make this tree work.

When we arrived home, Steve took charge, barking orders like a drill sergeant. "John, get my saw. If I lop off a few of these bottom branches and trim the trunk maybe we'll be able to slide it through without taking the door off the hinges. Jim, hold the door open. Edie, help your mother get dinner ready."

An hour later, I brought my husband a plate of spaghetti and a warm cup of coffee. He took a sip and shook his head, as he eyed the monstrosity spread out on the living room floor. "Phase one completed. You know I love you," he said.

Translated, he meant, "You're nuts, woman."

He looked around. "Where is this twig going?"

I pointed to the dining room, and Steve shook his head. I quickly realized the tree was still three feet too tall.

My husband thrives on challenge. "John, get me the saw again. This is the tree your mother wants and this is where it's going." After a few more adjustments, he hoisted it into the stand, not even flinching when it toppled. But my valiant knight managed to keep it upright by tying it to the frame of the suspended ceiling. Like a maniacal marionette without a puppeteer, its arms engulfed the entire dining room.

After everything we'd endured, I began to despise what I thought I'd treasure. Its initial attraction was lost in its present grotesque state. If money hadn't been so tight, we'd have thrown it out and started anew with a nursery tree from Kmart.

Because there was now no room for our table, we ate our meals standing up or on TV trays in the living room. With every bite, I growled at the tree, flooded with regret for putting my family through such major inconvenience.

There was nothing I could do but make the best of an uncomfortable situation. I had learned my lesson and vowed to do things differently next year. Over the next few days, we added lights and ornaments. Maybe we simply got used to looking at it, but eventually the thing became a part of our existence, its presence like an unattractive friend, a beauty hidden beneath the layers of distraction.

On Christmas Eve, we piled the presents under what we had affectionately dubbed The Beast. As Edie examined the wrapped packages, she scanned the tree, her head cocked and her face pensive. Then she asked, "Can we sing Christmas carols?" Steve grabbed the guitar while Edie turned off the house lights.

Then a miracle happened. During "Silent Night," all seemed calm and bright. With its broad branches, the lights exuded a halo effect, adding angelic chords to our rendition. I could almost see the shepherds as they knelt in wonder at the Savior's birth.

Was it just me or had the tree finally completed a metamorphosis, transformed from an object of ridicule to a thing of beauty? I thought about our Savior's sacrifice – willing to become an object of scorn – and the ugliness of the cross, beautiful to those who believe.

In that moment, I realized the hope that caused me to select this very tree days before. Perhaps I'd chosen it not for what it was then, but for what it would become: a symbol of sacrificial love.

"Look at that!" Edie cried. "We couldn't see how pretty it was in the daytime. It took night to make it glow!"

That was the message God gave us that Christmas Eve. *"The light shines in the darkness, but the darkness has not understood it... The Word became flesh and made his dwelling among us. We have seen his glory, the glory of the One and Only, who came from the Father, full of grace and truth."* (John 1:5,14 NIV)

From that year on, singing Christmas carols around the tree became an integral part of our holiday celebrations until one-by-one the children left home and began their own family traditions. Long distances between us made holiday trips a rare occurrence. Still, whether on the cards we sent or during holiday phone calls, we often reminisced about The Beast and that special Christmas Eve.

A few years ago, we visited Edie, now a mother of three, busy housewife and successful accountant, during the Christmas holiday. Our grandson, then aged eight, having heard the story of the miracle tree, asked his grandfather to bring his guitar on this visit so we could sing Christmas carols around their tree like his mother did when she was a little girl. Of course, the guitar was the first thing packed as we loaded the car for our journey.

The decorations were different, and my daughter's store-bought tree more refined than the one that consumed our dining room years ago. Yet, when the lights were turned off and the music started, I felt as if I'd been taken back to that time.

I reflected on all the miracles God had allowed in my life, overflowing with gratitude for all God has done in spiritually transforming my life over the years. I thanked him for the gift of Jesus, wrapped in commonness for the beauty of all mankind to behold.

~ *Linda Wood Rondeau*

❦ 24 ❦

Granny's Dishes

My mind raced as I trudged through the mall with my holiday shopping list. How did Christmas get so hectic? Sometimes I think I'd like to skip it.

"Oh, Father, forgive me," I whispered. "It's not that I don't want to celebrate the birth of Jesus. I just dread going into debt."

I thought back to Christmases when my children were small and the stacks of expensive gifts were wrapped in equally expensive wrappings I'd always provided. Back then, I'd felt I had to get everything on their Santa Claus lists, and, of course, I had to compete with their grandparents' gifts. Continuing the tradition into their adulthood, I used credit cards to provide them with lavish Christmas gifts...and my expenses added up to a total somewhere near the national debt. Well, maybe not that much, but let's just say it took me months to pay off. As a result Christmas had become a burden instead of a joy.

"Lord, please help me get my joy back," I prayed. "Christmas should be about celebrating your gift to us through the birth of Jesus Christ, not what I've made it. How can I make it right?"

I paused to admire a window display of holiday tableware and remembered a Christmas long ago when my grandmother was still alive.

Granny's birthday was in December. That year the family had gathered in her church's fellowship hall to celebrate her 80th birthday. We had met there because none of us lived in a house big enough for the whole family. Granny birthed eleven children and mothered four stepchildren. With nine of her children still living and the second and third generations in attendance, we had numbered close to a hundred.

The family had come together to bless and celebrate Granny, but that Christmas, Granny surprised us all with a gift for every family represented. "I'm sorry I can't give every one of you a present, but I just want you all to know how much I love you." Her thin, frail voice broke with emotion and love shone brightly from her faded blue eyes.

Granny passed out her gifts, wrapped in obviously recycled white tissue paper and tied with red curling ribbon. We opened them to find a bowl, a plate, or a cup. All were dime store dishes with a pretty, pale-pink rose decal and gold trimmed edges. Her joy made her face glow as she watched us open them. Even though the dishes cost less than a dollar apiece, I knew she sacrificed to give them and I loved her very much for that.

Through the years I treasured my little dime-store dish, and every time I used it, I thought of Granny's love. The dish reminded me that giving – not the cost – is the important thing. Several years later, I dropped the bowl and broke it beyond repair. I lost a prized possession that day, and along with it, Granny's valuable lesson about the joy of giving.

I tore my shopping list into little pieces. "Oh, Father, I promise to change how I celebrate Christmas. I'm so sorry I never told my children that story. And I'm sorry for my part in making Christmas all about expensive presents. Please help me find some of Granny's dishes and give me the chance to tell them about her lesson."

My faith was weak in thinking God might answer the prayer the way I asked it. This was forty years after Granny had given her dishes. In all my years of going to garage sales and flea markets, I'd never run across any of the dishes.

I checked some internet sites but came up empty.

The following Saturday, I headed out to the garage sales, again praying the whole time to find some of Granny's dishes. After making the rounds with no success, I headed for the local flea market.

There on the table before me sat a whole stack of Granny's dishes: four cereal bowls, two dinner plates, and a beautiful platter. A couple of the bowls were chipped, but that was okay, because I'd keep them for myself.

I became so excited I almost paid full price, but got control of myself just in time. After some good-natured haggling, the dealer and I reached a price comfortable for us both. As I handed over my cash, I whispered a happy, "Thank you Lord," and marveled at God's generosity in answering my prayer. "Oh, Father, you always go above and beyond what I could ask or think.

Thank you so much!"

Later, I sang Christmas carols as I wrapped the plates and bowls in white tissue paper with red curling ribbon, just like Granny's. When finished I prayed, "Father, going forward, please help me to always focus on gifts from the heart. And please remind me to stay within my means."

On Christmas day, I gave the plates and bowls to each of my daughters. As they opened the boxes, I told them the story of Granny's dishes. I told them I wanted to follow Granny's example, and that going forward my gifts would be simple, like the dishes, and always from my heart.

I suspected my radical change was a big surprise to my daughters that Christmas. I wondered if my children were touched by the lesson I had tried to impart. I knew that only time would tell if the lesson of Granny's dishes would affect the girls like it did me.

Later, on a visit to my daughter's home, I saw that she had not thrown away the dish, nor hidden it away in a cupboard. She'd hung the dish in a prominent place on her kitchen wall.

We smiled at each other. With great joy I prayed, "Thank you for hearing my prayer, Father. You helped me find the dishes, and I know you'll do the rest."

Every morning, when I take my chipped cereal bowl with the faded pink roses from the cupboard, I remember Granny's lesson about love and giving.

I can visualize Granny's Christmas lesson becoming a family tradition of remembering the most valuable presents don't depend upon the cost, but whether they're given from a heart of love – like God's present to us.

~ Gail Griner Golden

25

Christmas Treat

My Pomeranian, Rigel, always jumps up the minute I go to my office and set my cup of coffee on the side table. He sits close to me with front arms and paws on the windowsill and looks out while I read aloud from the Bible and devotional book and pray.

This Christmas morning as I sat on the big overstuffed chair, my tabby cat, Sabby, jumped up into my lap, closer than usual to Rigel. Fortunately, my rescue dog was well-trained and "stays" when I say so.

Just as we three were settled and I had begun reading the Bible, the phone rang. Suspecting who it was, I rose to go to the bedroom for the phone. The cat jumped to the floor. The dog followed on my heels.

As my daughter, her husband, and their thirteen-year-old son began singing "We Wish You a Merry Christmas," I held the phone between the two animals. They moved away in opposite directions. I laughed, enjoying the frivolity.

After "Merry Christmas" and "I love you" from each side, I settled in again on the chair, my heart cheerful. I thought about the plans for the day. On Christmas Eve some of my family had gone to a worship service at church. This afternoon some of the family would come and we would have finger foods and watch the movie, *Star of Bethlehem*. Later, other family members would come and we'd have the turkey I'd cook, and all the trimmings they'd bring. We would laugh and fight over Dirty Santa, play our Alphabet Gift game, and exchange presents.

I thought of what I'd taught my children when they were growing up…that we show our love to each other by giving, whether it's an expensive gift or a handmade card, because God showed his love to us by giving.

I looked at my pets who had returned to sit with me as I continued with my devotions for the day, which included the Bible's Christmas story of Jesus' birth. I thought about Rigel and Sabby and how I believe they love me, but so often I feel they just try to please me to get a treat.

That led me to think about how my actions appear to God. Am I always asking him for treats? He's given me the greatest treat – Jesus coming, living, dying, resurrecting for my sins so I can have inner peace on earth and an eternal home in heaven.

So this Christmas morning I decided to do what my daughter and her family had done for me. They had wished me a Merry Christmas and told me they loved me. So during my prayer time, I did not ask for anything, nor tell God what treats I wanted. Instead, I thanked him for what he has already given, wished God and Jesus a Merry Christmas and told Jesus I hoped he had a Happy Birthday celebration.

What better present could we have than what God has already given? The gift is here. We just need to accept it. What a Christmas (and forever) treat!

~ Yvonne Lehman

… 26 …

A Christmas to Remember

I had spent days preparing and packing for all ten of us to make this trip. At the airport while my husband went to check in, I tried to keep track of the children plus all the coats and sweaters that would be needed at our destination – but were seldom worn in South Florida.

Finally we boarded the plane.

It was difficult to contain the children's excitement. They bounced around in their seats and argued over who would sit by the window next. We did make it through dinner, however, without a major mishap. Afterward, the flight attendants, dressed as Santas, passed through the cabin with candies, wishing each person "Merry Christmas."

Eventually exhaustion overwhelmed the excitement, and the children fell asleep. "What an unusual way to celebrate Christmas Eve," I thought.

The jumbo jet rushed through the night skies en route to Victoria, British Columbia, where we would visit with my husband's family.

The plane was virtually empty, so I had room to stretch out, alone with my thoughts. Placing the small Walkman earphones in my ears, I listened to the Christmas carol cassettes I had slipped into my carry-on bag at the last minute. Soon their beautiful, familiar strains filled my whole being with the wonder of this special season.

I looked down upon the earth 36,000 feet below and watched one small snow-covered town after another pass beneath us. As their lights twinkled and glistened off the snow, I wondered how those people were celebrating this night.

I'm usually frantic on Christmas Eve. I sit on the floor wrapping gifts until late, asking myself questions: Have I done everything? Will the children be disappointed? Is the turkey defrosted? Did I make enough pot pies? Where are the stockings? How am I going to convince my husband to put together one more toy?

If my husband were to ask me what I most wanted for Christmas, I would likely reply, "Peace and quiet."

And now I had it.

Gazing at the towns and hamlets gliding by below, I wondered how many others felt as I did on most Christmas Eves. Were they rushing around now doing last-minute shopping, frayed and frustrated because the toy store failed to get another shipment of the latest children's craze? Were they dreading disappointment on Christmas morning? Were they worn out? Harried? Did they long for a good night of rest and a day of peace and quiet?

As the majestic music continued to soothe my soul, I prayed for those below, beleaguered by their blessings. Just before we landed, I woke the children. Quickly gathering our belongings and stuffing ourselves into coats and jackets, we hurried to greet family members we hadn't seen for some time, then made our way to the hotel.

It was late when finally I tucked each small child into bed, making sure he or she was warm enough. Later, as I lay recuperating in a warm bath, I reflected on the fact that although I was tired and weary I was not completely worn out. I was fatigued but not utterly frazzled. I wondered why. Could it be that, despite everything, this Christmas Eve was simpler?

I pulled on a warm robe and went to look out the window. What a charming town. So different from South Florida, where we celebrate Christmas in sundresses and sandals, and decorate palm trees instead of evergreens.

I opened the window, careful not to wake my husband, and felt the cold, fresh air rush in. Then I crawled between crisp, white sheets, and with a thankful heart, fell asleep.

On Christmas morning I awoke to the aroma of fresh coffee. A moment or two later, my husband entered our room with a steaming cup and a cheery "Christmas gift!" (We follow an old family tradition of seeing who can be the first to say "Christmas gift" on Christmas morning.) We dressed and went down to breakfast. Soon our tummies were satisfied.

I decided to take the children off to explore the town. It was a glorious Christmas Day. It definitely felt cold for us thin-blooded Floridians, but the sun was bright and the sky brilliant blue.

We walked along the port, watching the boats bobbing in the gentle waves. We passed the Parliament building and the museum. We glanced through the doorways of cozy tearooms and peeked into cleverly decorated shop windows. We walked up and down the small, quaint streets, wondering how those behind the doors of the charming cottages were celebrating this Christmas morning.

Soon we came upon a large, picturesque hotel that dominated one side of the port. Beginning to feel the bite of cold air, we decided to go in and investigate. Instructing the children to behave and reminding them of their manners, I shepherded them into the lobby. I heard music and noticed people assembling in front of the large fireplace. I quickly found a big winged chair, sat down and gathered the children around me.

An ensemble of men and women dressed in historical costumes walked into the room. They began to sing Christmas carols, and for over half an hour they sang one familiar favorite after another. Sitting there before the open fire, surrounded by all my children and listening to carols on this special morning, I was overcome by emotion.

For me this was Christmas.

No hustle and bustle, no hurry and haste, no stress and strains, no fruitless frustrations. Just warmth, love, family, and a quiet, peaceful heart overflowing with gratefulness. What more could a mother ask for?

All too soon the singing was over, and we found ourselves once again bundling up against the cold. It was nearly time for lunch, so we made our way back to our hotel. Over hot soup, thick bread, and tangy cider, sharing our discoveries with my husband, I experienced a warm sense of contentment.

The afternoon passed quickly and we hurried to ready ourselves for Christmas celebrations with my husband's family. Soon all ten of us joined all ten of them in their apartment for a delightful (if sometimes noisy) evening.

Because they were not yet in their new home, my husband's parents had kept things simple: a simple tree, a simple meal, and simple gifts. But we made up for it with lots of happy chatter and confusion.

I sat on the end of the sofa, observing the joyful chaos, watching everyone laugh at the antics of our toddler. I listened to all the aunts and uncles talking with our teenagers. I looked at my husband's elderly father and mother simply enjoying the happy commotion of being surrounded by their large family. I noticed how much the children were reveling in all the love, attention, and acceptance of the extended family. I saw my husband observing it all and glimpsed the parental pride in his eyes.

We ate dinner, opened our few gifts, then gathered to share the Christmas story. *For unto you is born this day in the city of David a Saviour, which is Christ the Lord.* (Luke 2:11)

This is the often-forgotten treasure, I thought. Simply that we have a Savior.

Later that night while tucking each child into bed, I thanked the Lord for reminding me again that the real celebration of his birth is not in the temporary pleasure found in the tinsel and toys…nor in the transient satisfaction of lovely gifts…nor in the brief display of magnificent decorations…nor in the fleeting enjoyment of delicious food.

The real meaning of Christmas is found not in the ephemeral, but in the eternal.

Why do I forget this year after year? Why is it that I usually think of Christmas with dread? Surely this was not the way it was meant to be.

True Christmas was more like what I had experienced that day: love and sharing, being together and doing for others, finding joy in giving to him the gift of ourselves.

In the still darkness of the night I thought, "I must try to understand just why Christmas has become so chaotic for me."

Could I be too caught up in the expectations of others? Am I afraid of disappointing or letting someone down? Are others really expecting so much of me, or am I imposing these expectations and pressures on my perfectionist self?

One way I could cope and change would be to deliberately decide not to try to fulfill each wish and expectation. I could choose two or three pressures that I would determine to eliminate. Would my friends really be offended if they didn't receive a Christmas card this year? Maybe I could send Easter cards instead.

Would the children really be disappointed if we gave fewer gifts or decorated a smaller tree? Would the neighbors truly mind if I gave them a small ornament instead of a bag of home-baked goodies?

I don't want to dampen all the traditions and expectations of the holiday season, but I do want to make sure my priorities are in the right order. I want time to think about the real meaning of Christmas, time to concentrate my energy and efforts on people in the community and their concerns…instead of tinsel and temporal things.

Decorations and festivities are wonderful ways to commemorate the birth of a loved one, but I thought how terribly hurt I would be if on my birthday everyone was so busy getting ready to celebrate that no one remembered me.

Surely the Lord, too, must enjoy the time we spend with him. Time alone in quiet meditation, time together in worshipful praise and thanksgiving.

I soon fell asleep with praise on my lips and thanksgiving in my heart for all that this special Christmas had brought to me. Somewhere beneath all the temporal trappings, the true, timeless treasure still waits to be found.

Come…and behold Him!

~ *Gigi Graham*

❧ 27 ❧

Christmas Hopes and Fears

Two days before Thanksgiving, the dermatologist found a lump in our daughter Anita's leg. Her previous melanoma surgery as a newlywed meant she would need a biopsy. It seemed such gloomy news, particularly with Christmas so near.

As I lay awake nights, tossing and turning, I pleaded with God, "Please, no more cancer for Anita."

I remembered a friend's remark before Anita's surgery two years earlier. "Don't let the enemy steal your joy."

I wanted a joyful Christmas season. If I spent the weeks before the biopsy worrying, I'd accomplish nothing and miss that joy. I decided to expect a good report. If it wasn't, there would be time for tears later.

Our son called to discuss holiday plans. "What do you want for Christmas?" he asked.

"Thanks for asking," I said. "But it's nothing anyone can buy. All I want is a healthy daughter."

In the meantime, what could I do? I prayed, and shared my concerns with friends who prayed. I knew God was loving and good, so I tried to trust him. I told myself he loved Anita more than I did and he knew best.

Anita's surgery day finally arrived. That afternoon she called to say, "They removed the lump. I saw it." She laughed. "It looked like chicken fat. I'll get the lab results on Thursday."

That evening I served a festive dinner using our best china. My husband and I celebrated our hopeful news with guarded optimism. I wanted…no, I needed…conclusive evidence from the pathology report to feel assured.

Thursday came, and I continued to pray for a good report. Halfheartedly, I went to the mall to buy Christmas gifts. Seasonal music played in the background, perhaps unnoticed by busy, noisy shoppers. But, above the din, I heard the words from a familiar carol in a new way. "The hopes and fears of all the years are met in thee tonight." Yes, I knew about hopes and fears. They tumbled and churned inside me. It would take God's help to put aside my fears and focus on hope.

Returning home, I listened to my phone messages. None from Anita. Was the news so bad she didn't want to tell me? I busied myself cooking dinner.

The phone interrupted me. "Hi, Mom, no news yet. I'll call the doctor again tomorrow."

Another day? More fears crowded in. No! I needed to trust God. No matter what the outcome, he would see us through. I knew family and friends were praying, and I felt God's peace return.

The next morning, I shopped for my last gifts, knowing I couldn't buy the gift I really wanted. Only Jesus, whose birth we would soon celebrate, could ease my fears. He alone could give me hope and peace whether or not my daughter had cancer. I prayed for hope. I prayed for peace. Once again, God calmed my heart.

I hurried home, but found no message from Anita. More waiting. When the phone rang, I picked it up and heard Anita say, "The doctor said everything is fine."

"Thank God!" I said. "That's what I was hoping for." I sat down by the kitchen table and cried in relief and gratitude.

Six days remained before Christmas, but God had already given me the only gift I wanted. I bowed my head and thanked him for a healthy daughter.

~ Lydia E. Harris

The rest of the story…

In the sixteen years since that Christmas, I've found God faithful and trustworthy during times of health challenges and fears. He hasn't always answered prayers as I hoped, but I've sensed his loving care, compassion, and grace as he walked through difficulties with me.

As I celebrate another Christmas with my family, I thank God for his constant presence during the good times and the challenging seasons of life. He reminded me years ago in the mall that all my hopes and fears are met in him.

May the God of hope fill you with all joy and peace as you trust in him, so that you may overflow with hope by the power of the Holy Spirit.
Romans 15:13 (NIV)

An Unforgettable Christmas Eve

I stared out the front window of our new home. The snow forecast made me feel apprehensive. All of my life I had lived in Scottsdale, Arizona where it is dry, desert, cacti landscaped, and the winters are warm enough to go swimming.

My husband and I had talked over what we wanted for our family. A highway patrol officer, he had purposefully taken a transfer so we could raise our daughter in a smaller town.

Now we lived in Eagar, Arizona only five hours from Scottsdale but a place where one could snow ski. Towering pine trees, meadows, brooks, and lakes surrounded our new home.

My mind raced, filled with thoughts of Scottsdale. One question repeated itself over and over. "How will I ever survive Christmas without my family, friends, and convenience of the big city?"

By November, Scottsdale glittered with the promise of the Christmas season. Storefronts sparkled with colored lights, wrapped presents, and the lure of the perfect gifts one should buy. Church programs brought joyful songs and praise to the birth of Jesus and kept parents busy sewing angel costumes for the tiny performers. On street corners, bells tinkled for donations. Volunteers kept busy putting together gift baskets for the needy. Year after year I looked forward to those activities.

This year however, by the time we were almost settled in the house, Christmas was upon us. We'd had no time to cut a tree and the small town was out of live ones. The town was sparsely decorated. We hadn't found a church, and we'd missed the Christmas parade the town holds several weeks before Christmas.

I quietly decorated an artificial tree, shopped in the one store in town, and tried to get used to the bitter cold.

My daughter, Lindsey, giggled every day in anticipation of the white stuff.

She hounded me, "When is it going to snow?" She so wanted to play in piles of snow that forecasters assured us would happen by Christmas.

We lit the pellet stove and snuggled together on the couch. Christmas carols played on the radio. We resigned ourselves to a quiet Christmas Eve, just the three of us along with our Golden Retriever and Saint Bernard that lay curled at our feet.

When the doorbell rang, I hoped to open the door to the sound of carolers, something I had always loved when we lived in Scottsdale. Instead, Wendell, the only neighbor we knew so far, stood at the door. His smile reached the corners of his eyes. "Hey, we just wondered if you, hubby and your little girl would like to join us in our traditional Christmas Eve hay ride."

Caught off guard, I stammered. "Uh, uh, well, I guess so. Yes."

I turned and looked into Ray's wide-eyed expression. He stood nodding his head up and down. Lindsey jumped around like a kangaroo. "Can we? Can we go, Mom? Pleeeese."

We dressed quickly in warm clothing and joined Wendell on the porch. We piled in his car. It slowly meandered down a narrow dirt road and stopped in front of a roaring bonfire. Twenty or more neighbors surrounded its blaze. A horse-drawn wagon stood off to the side already filled with laughing children, teens, and adults.

Total strangers hugged us and men slapped Ray on his back and shook his hand. A group of young people handed out cups of hot chocolate and warm donuts. The sky seemed bigger and the stars shone brighter than I'd ever seen. A group of teens strummed "Silent Night" on their guitars and a flutist played alongside them.

Tears fought their way past my eyelashes. They fell softly on my cheeks. Children surrounded Lindsey. They grabbed her hands and pulled her into game play. Before long she roasted her first marshmallow on a straightened wire clothes hanger and enjoyed her first S'more.

"All aboard!" someone shouted. We squashed shoulder-to-shoulder onto the hay wagon. The fresh scent of new-cut hay tickled my nose. The driver, a burly cowboy wearing a huge hat pulled down over his ears, hollered, "On Donnor!" He snapped a long whip and we lurched ahead.

We arrived at a scene that took my breath away. A lit stable with a live nativity brought my trickle of tears to a flood. Three young women played violins with precision and calm grace. "Oh, Come All Ye Faithful" floated on the still night air. Baby Jesus cooed in the arms of a young Mary. A deep voice flowed from behind the enclosure that represented the manger. "And to you this night, a babe is born. He will be called Jesus."

Suddenly, I knew that God had placed us right where he wanted us for this season in our lives. Yes, we missed our family and friends we'd left behind for this new adventure. But these people presented a promise of new friendships, new beginnings and memories that could last a lifetime.

That Christmas Eve in Eagar, Arizona presented a new truth to me. Good things can come through change and trial. Fretting over a change is a waste of precious time.

God has a plan for me and my family, and I now cherish those new relationships that enrich my life.

~ Alice Klies

29

The Best Christmas Ever

Like most children I loved the Christmas season. Those three or four weeks leading up to Christmas were so special I never wanted them to end.

Colored lights, wreaths, garland, candles, and beautiful homemade decorations adorned the outside and inside of our house – den, living room, hallways, kitchen, dining room, every bedroom and even all six bathrooms.

My favorite place was our recreation room. We played pinball, shuffleboard and darts. The adults gathered around the bar, the piano, or the jukebox singing, laughing, hugging and kissing each other.

The ping pong and pool tables overflowed with many kinds of delicious meats, casseroles and sweets. There were always two huge bowls of punch – one for us kids and one for the adults.

Sometimes we were even able to bowl, but usually the lane was filled with big presents that were special gifts from Santa for Mom, Dad or relatives.

My sister and I considered that room our Magic Kingdom. We could hardly wait to open our presents. Sometimes wrapped packages were piled halfway up the Christmas tree.

I loved that holiday so much I often pretended it was Christmas during the spring, summer and fall. In fact, I remember one July I asked, "Mommy, could we celebrate Christmas for a little bit right now? I could go with Daddy and we could chop down a Christmas tree and then all of us decorate it."

She laughed, hugged me and said, "No, Silly-Willy. Santa's reindeer and Mr. & Mrs. Claus take their vacation now."

I loved ice cream, and Christmas meant having the best tasting ice creams available, like spumoni – and my favorite, winter white chocolate. It tasted like a super duper banana split on steroids. Boy, was it delicious!

As I grew a little older my memories of past Christmases were replaced with new ones. We still ate ice cream, but instead of remembering how good it tasted, I now remembered Dad getting angry and throwing it across the kitchen table at Mom. The glass bowl broke and ice cream splattered on us, the table, and the floor. Yelling, screaming, and swearing followed.

Eventually the fighting escalated. Dad became more violent and abusive. Mom and Dad stopped having parties. The laughter, singing and hugging I had associated with Christmas ended. We still received presents, but smiles were replaced with ugly facial expressions. Former verbal expressions like "I love you" were replaced with words that were meant to hurt.

Then one Christmas was strangely different. The owner of the company where my dad worked invited our family to a party. He told those gathered that Dad was one of the best salesmen in the country and that he made the company lots of money. Everyone applauded. That made us happy for Dad. He seemed happy then, too.

The rest of the party was different from anything I'd ever experienced. They sang Christmas carols. The words were beautiful and peaceful. When they sang, "I'm Dreaming of a White Christmas," I wished my family's Christmas would be like it used to be.

We sang "Away in the Manager" and a song about a Little Drummer Boy. Then our host told a story about baby Jesus.

I sat there listening to every word. As I listened I felt a chill, as if little goose bumps were running up and down my body.

He talked about Jesus becoming an adult. He said Jesus Christ helped lots of people. He then shared how some men became very jealous of Jesus and said things about him that were not true; they even talked about killing him. He said Jesus was nailed to a cross, died, but came alive again.

I had never heard stories like that. Dad was an atheist. But I could tell the man who spoke that night at the company Christmas party knew Jesus, and they were buddies.

Eventually Dad and Mom divorced. It was nearly ten years before I learned how I could know Jesus personally. I had to wait such a long time to learn more about Jesus because the people I hung around with did not know Jesus. Or, if they did, they never told me about him.

When I reflect on past Christmases now, I realize that the best and most important Christmas I ever had was when I first heard of Jesus.

I wish my dad had understood that story.

As I've grown older I've learned that it is possible to celebrate the birth of Christ any day of the week for fifty-two straight weeks by telling others about Jesus.

Because I wondered why I had to wait so many years before somebody told me why Jesus was born, every day I try to tell somebody the story I heard years and years ago.

I often pray that others will share, because there are thousands of little boys, girls, moms, and dads who have never heard, but need and want to hear the story of Jesus.

As we begin making a list of Christmas gifts we want to give to others, we need to remember to add the most special gift – the story of Christmas and the gift God has given us.

It's God's way of saying, "Merry Christmas to you…and you…and you."

- Tommy Scott Gilmore, III

30

Where Did Prince Charming Go?

He opened his Christmas gifts first, then dancing with anticipation handed me my present. The gift bag was securely closed with a ridge of scotch tape, evidence of his own hand in this artful presentation. I exercised all the pre-opening rituals: gently stroking the outside, carefully shaking it near the ear, and complimenting the packaging, as well as the obligatory, "Thank you, Honey." I even ventured a few guesses.

In an instant, I popped the row of scotch tape and looked inside the satiny red wrapping bag. I froze in disbelief as I stared at what my husband deemed the perfect gift.

A shower massage!

I knew right then and there the romance was more than dead. It was beyond resuscitation. In fact, it was stone cold.

"For me?" I feigned pleasure.

Since we had bought a video camera as a mutual Christmas present to each other, we'd set a personal gift limit of $25. He went over the top to $30.

"You shouldn't have," I said…honestly.

At some point over the past couple of decades, the Prince Charming I married had gone through a metamorphosis. The handsome suitor who used to buy me chocolates emerged as an aged athlete peddling coffee. Practicality had slowly replaced sentimentality. I wanted to tell my one-time hero to take a hike, then find my misplaced fairy godmother and tell her to bring back Prince Charming.

"Pour yourself another cup of coffee and relax," he said, "while I get the shower massage ready for you." He took the monstrosity from the bag, and with his toolbox in hand, bounded up the steps like a schoolboy at recess.

He whistled while he worked. In the meantime, I stewed in my disappointment. "A shower massage. Humph!" I felt like Grumpy while he played the part of Happy.

"All set," he beamed. "You first! After all, it is your present."

"That it is." I trudged to the upstairs bathroom, took off my robe, and stepped into the widespread spray. To my pleasant surprise, the steamy mist enveloped my senses. I felt as if I had just entered a sauna.

"Well, now. This is sort of nice." I took the showerhead in hand and experimented with the dial. Suddenly, streams of pulsating gushes hit my arthritic joints. I let my mind drift, imagining I was under a waterfall in Tahiti. Hey, I thought. This is not bad. Not bad at all.

When there was no more hot water, I reluctantly turned the shower off, towel-dried, put on my bathrobe, and wandered downstairs.

My Joe DiMaggio was anxiously awaiting the umpire's verdict. "Well?" He looked like an innocent child who had just given his mother a wilted dandelion, waiting for a hug of gratitude.

He smiled his cute little boy smile. Behind the grin, I recognized the faded but familiar royalty that I had fallen in love with so many years before. My once darling Prince Charming still lived inside that paunchy but adorable man, and he knew exactly what kind of Christmas present this tired, achy body needed.

- Linda Wood Rondeau

≈ 31 ≈

My Favorite Childhood Christmas

"Little people have big ears." I heard my aunts whisper that to my Mom more than once. I earned the distinction by hiding behind a door, chair, or tree in order to gain more information.

At seven, well experienced at ferreting out secrets, I knew that Daddy, along with several dozen other townspeople, had been called up by the Selective Service. Then the announcement came that the war had ended. Daddy said when they were given the choice to stay and be sworn in or to leave, the place emptied in seconds.

I heard the whispers about lack of money, every penny counting, and Mom whispering something about what she would like to do for Christmas.

I thought that might mean there would be no presents. But, if we only had a Christmas tree, I'd be happy.

In other years Dad had brought home a tree to decorate with paper chains and strings of popcorn. But this year Dad and Mom started a store in the living room. They replaced the sofa with a big freezer chest, then added a counter with bins on the front. It was so crowded there was no room for anything else. Certainly not a Christmas tree.

I'd heard the deliveryman whisper to Daddy that he hoped a television would work to get people to come to our little store. It did, likely because it was the first TV in town. It seemed the entire population of 500 came to see it. Most people purchased something while there.

Because Mom and Dad said every penny went to get the TV and to have the store stocked, I was sure there would be no Christmas at our house that year.

We followed our tradition of going to the midnight church service on Christmas Eve. I loved seeing mysterious dark trees, decorated with blue lights, rising from the Nativity scene to the ceiling of the church.

After being up so late, we children slept longer than usual Christmas morning. After awakening, my sister, brother and I tiptoed down the stairs just in case Christmas had come. We were dumbfounded to discover the door to our former living room, now grocery store, firmly locked.

We banged on the door until Mom's voice on the other side said she would unlock the door after we sang some Christmas carols. It was fun to each start our favorite, be joined by the others, and then ask, "Now?" We knew something had to be on the other side of that door.

After each song, Mom would say, "That was so pretty – just one more." Finally after Mom's favorite, "O Christmas Tree," the key turned, and the door slowly swung open.

We gasped. Mom was standing in snow. Snow inside the house!

Behind her were footprints, seemingly made by giant boots. Santa? We carefully obeyed her direction to follow the footprints. We filed through the store, around the counter, past shelves and cooler, into the hall by the downstairs bedroom and into the kitchen.

Apparently Santa had been here. He must have been looking for the tree that wasn't there.

Finally, the footsteps ended by the back door. In a mound of snow in the center of the backyard stood the smallest tree from the nativity at church.

Dad had provided trees for the church and arranged to bring home the little one after the service. Our excited "Ohhhh!" acknowledged the beautiful and unexpected gift.

Mom interrupted our admiration of the lovely sight. "After you open your stockings," she said, "you can make suet balls and decorate the tree." She pointed behind us to the decorations we'd missed.

We retraced our steps, cheering as we raced to the three stockings hanging on the back of the counter in the living room. We'd passed so near them, unseeing, in our excitement to follow the footprints!

I do not recall what was in the stockings except for fruit and nuts. I remember opening a present, but I was more eager to return to the kitchen where we rolled chunks of suet in peanut butter, then tiny seeds, tied the bird-treats with red ribbons then hung them on the little tree.

It was a beautiful sight. It wasn't long before Christmas birds showed up for their holiday treat. While we ate lunch, and later played board games and worked puzzles, we would each steal out to the back door to watch the tree alive with birds enjoying their Christmas treats.

I hadn't heard one whisper about the snow. It was years later before I learned the snow we so enjoyed was really flour. But that year, it was Christmas inside and out! The happiest Christmas of my childhood.

~ *Delores Liesner*

❦ 32 ❦

A Partridge in a Pear Tree?
The Meaning of a Christmas Carol

This arrived in an email to a writers loop, but I don't have the name of the sender. It may or may not be true but whoever wrote it obviously gave it a lot of thought and meaning. The sender wrote: "The Twelve Days of Christmas" is one Christmas carol that has always baffled me. What in the world do leaping lords, French hens, swimming swans, and especially the partridge who won't come out of the pear tree have to do with Christmas?

This week, I found out.

From 1558 until 1829, Roman Catholics in England were not permitted to practice their faith openly. During that era, someone wrote this carol as a catechism song for young Catholics, with each day's gift representing an aspect of the Christian faith.

- The partridge in a pear tree is Jesus Christ.
- Two turtle doves represent the Old and New Testaments.
- Three French hens stand for faith, hope and love.
- Four calling birds are the four gospels of Matthew, Mark, Luke, and John.
- Five golden rings recall the Torah or Law, the first five books of the Old Testament.
- Six geese a-laying stand for the six days of creation.
- Seven swans a-swimming represent the sevenfold gifts of the Holy Spirit – prophecy, serving, teaching, exhortation, contribution, leadership, and mercy.
- Eight maids a-milking are the eight beatitudes.
- Nine ladies dancing are the nine fruits of the Holy Spirit – love, joy, peace, patience, kindness, goodness, faithfulness, gentleness, and self-control.

- Ten lords a-leaping are the Ten Commandments.
- Eleven pipers piping stand for the eleven faithful disciples.
- Twelve drummers drumming symbolize the twelve points of belief in the Apostles' Creed.

The email sender wrote: This was shared with me and I found it interesting and enlightening. Now I know how that strange song became a Christmas Carol. Pass it on if you wish. "Merry Christmas Everyone."

~ Anonymous

33
A Comedy of Errors

My fiancée, June, and I were excited to learn that I would be granted four days' leave at Christmas. Finally, we could get married.

I was an airman stationed at Goodfellow Air Force Base in San Angelo, Texas. June lived with her mother in Searcy, Arkansas, where she attended Harding College. We had been engaged for two years and anxiously awaited such an opportunity. We felt our prayers had been answered.

June wished to get married in eastern Ohio where she grew up. Her Christmas vacation would allow her to get there about a week before Christmas. With the help of two sisters living in Ohio, she felt she could pull together a simple wedding in the time available.

That year, Christmas was on Thursday. I would have from Wednesday noon to midnight Sunday to travel to Ohio, get married, take care of a few incidentals, then return to the base at the end of four days. No sweat.

Or so I thought!

San Angelo's airport was served by one small airline with a limited number of flights each day. At Christmastime that presented a huge problem. When I contacted the airline a few weeks before Christmas, every flight had long been filled and had an impossible waiting list.

I booked a flight from Dallas to Pittsburgh, the major airport nearest to June's home and prayed for a way to get from San Angelo to Dallas, a distance of more than 260 miles. Since I had no car, I hoped to find a ride with someone going that way, catch a bus, or as a last resort, hitchhike. My prayers were answered. Another airman agreed to give me a ride to the airport for a few dollars. What a relief! Surely, it would be smooth sailing after that.

Right.

The airman dropped me off at the airport at 5:00 p.m. My flight would leave Dallas at 10:00 p.m. I had the dubious pleasure of spending five hours in the airport, flying from Dallas to Atlanta, and a two-hour layover before catching my flight to Pittsburgh.

At long last, despite snow and slick runways, we landed in Pittsburgh at 7:00 a.m. on Thursday, Christmas morning. Two of June's brothers-in-law met me. But my luggage, including the clothes I expected to be married in the next day, hadn't made it to Pittsburgh. The airline personnel promised to call as soon as it arrived.

We drove for about an hour from the airport to the home of June's sister, Jenny. That pleased me because June was staying with Jenny and I had not seen June since leaving for basic training in September. Jenny had breakfast ready for us. We had little time to talk, however. Right after breakfast we needed to pick up my best man, Gary, at the Cleveland airport, ten miles farther away than Pittsburgh.

Gary's flight had landed in Pittsburgh en route to Cleveland, and his luggage had been left in Pittsburgh. We returned to Jenny's house only to learn the airline had called. My luggage had arrived in Pittsburgh. So, we were on the road again, the day was soon spent, and it was time for dinner. What a way to spend Christmas! Running from airport to airport to airport!

The driving wasn't over yet. June and I drove her mother's car twenty-five miles to Salem, Ohio to meet my family who were driving in from out of state.

During all our rushing back and forth on the road, my parents were having their own difficulties. They and my brother were traveling on Christmas Eve from southeast Missouri to western Kentucky to pick up my aunt and spend the night with her before continuing their journey. They expected to reach Salem, Ohio, by late afternoon on Christmas Day. However, they failed to anticipate the blizzard!

They reached my aunt's house without difficulty on Christmas Eve.

Mom was driving my parents' car. Dad was driving my car, which June and I would drive back to the Air Force Base in Texas…if we could ever get off the road long enough to get married!

However, heavy snow was already falling. They'd planned to be on the road by 6:00 a.m. on Christmas day, but when Dad woke up at 1:00 a.m. and looked outside, that changed. He informed Mom that several inches of snow had fallen and it was still coming down. They did not want to miss my wedding, so they loaded up my parents' car and all rode together, with Dad driving. They hoped conditions would improve.

Not a chance.

The roads continued to be covered with deep snow, but they crept along. They traveled hundreds of miles before reaching plowed roads. They managed to find a phone and let Jenny know that they would arrive later than expected, about 9:00 p.m.

June and I were pleased to have a little time alone, our first since September. Not long, however, because we left Jenny's at 8:00 p.m. for the Salem, Ohio hospital where we were to meet my family at 9:00 p.m. When they had not arrived by 10:00 p.m., we began to worry. We were almost frantic by the time they appeared after midnight. But they were safe!

After greeting my parents, June returned to Jenny's. I rode with my family and guided them to the home of Vivian and Herman, friends of June's family, where we would spend the night. It was after 1:00 a.m. when I got to bed, and I had to get up early since June would be picking me up in a few hours.

Yes, we knew it was supposed to be bad luck to see the bride before the wedding, but these were special circumstances. Besides, what else could possibly go wrong?

We had things to do that were absolutely essential. We'd had no previous opportunity to obtain a marriage license. Jenny had found out that the waiting period would be waived for service members and the courthouse would be open on December 26. We could get the license that morning and get married that night, no problem!

Sure.

I asked June to drive. Since she was raised in Ohio, I thought she would be more familiar with driving on snow-covered roads. We made it fifty feet down the driveway before getting stuck! Then she told me she had never driven on slick roads before.

We got the car free, but in helping us Herman severely twisted his ankle. That presented a problem since he was scheduled to walk June down the aisle and give her away in lieu of her deceased father.

What next?

We arrived at the courthouse in Lisbon, Ohio, told the clerk we wanted a marriage license, and that I was in the Air Force and understood the waiting period could be waived for military personnel.

She agreed, then asked for our form. We had no idea what she was talking about. The person who had spoken to Jenny had failed to inform her that Ohio required a particular form to be signed by the service member's commanding officer in order for the waiting period to be waived.

We had no idea what to do. Our wedding was scheduled for that night. People had traveled hundreds of miles from several states to be there. Some had risked their lives.

We felt a brief moment of relief when the clerk told us the judge could waive the requirement for The Form – until she added that he would be out of the office until after the first of the year.

We were in shock!

After a few moments, we decided we would go ahead and hold the ceremony that night. Then, we would get legally married by a chaplain back in Texas. Fortunately, the clerk saved the day. She decided she would issue the license and have the judge approve it when he returned.

What a relief! All was well…until the clerk threw us another curve.

She asked if the preacher was certified to perform weddings in Ohio. We had no idea, since he would be coming from West Virginia. June told her the preacher's name, and after a while the clerk confirmed that he was, indeed, authorized to perform weddings in Ohio. We had just cleared two major hurdles and, finally, it appeared that our wedding might actually take place.

But we were skeptical!

The wedding did take place at 7:30 that night. It went off without a hitch. Something went smoothly, for a change. What a surprise!

It was a simple ceremony at the church June had attended before leaving for college. My friend, Gary, was my best man. June's twin sister, Betty, was matron of honor. June wore the same wedding gown Betty had worn for her own wedding earlier that year. Betty wore the bridesmaid's dress June had worn as Betty's maid of honor.

Herman managed to limp down the aisle with June on his arm and give her away. I sleepwalked through the ceremony. This was Friday evening and I had slept only a few hours since Monday night. Somehow, I managed to repeat my vows, place the ring on June's finger, receive her ring on mine, and hear the preacher pronounce us husband and wife.

But our adventures were far from over.

After a reception in the church basement, June and I rode with my parents to Vivian and Herman's. We planned to change clothes there and take my parents' car to a motel a few miles away. Alas, June had left her suitcase in Betty's car. It contained the special nightie she bought for our wedding night. Anybody knows a girl can't honeymoon without her special nightie!

So, we waited.

When they did not arrive within half an hour, we considered going back to get the suitcase, but feared we might pass them on the way and not recognize their car in the dark. So, we kept on waiting.

They finally arrived with a good reason for their delay. However, we did not reach the motel until after midnight. I will say nothing further about our wedding night except that the wait was worth it. My bride was a vision of loveliness in that long-awaited nightie. She was the most beautiful sight I had ever seen, and she was mine.

Morning came much too soon. We got up about 3:30 a.m. and arrived at Herman's at 4:30 to ride back to Kentucky with my parents and pick up my car. Six of us were stuffed into Dad's Chevy Impala. June and I rode all day in the backseat with my teenaged brother…hardly the way we wished to spend our honeymoon.

At about 6:00 p.m., June and I loaded up my car and set off for Missouri and arrived at my parents' house at 9:30 p.m. We got a few hours sleep.

Yet, we still needed to make an early start the next day, which was Sunday. Feeling we had plenty of time for me to be back on base before midnight, we drove to Harding College to pick up some of June's possessions. We took our time getting back on the road, thinking we had time to spare.

Wrong again!

We planned to stop for dinner near Dallas, but our route took us near the

Cotton Bowl where the Cowboys were playing that day. Although the game had been over for a while by the time we got there, traffic was extremely heavy. We had no time for dinner since we had to reach the base by midnight or I'd be AWOL. We stopped at a gas station for Pepsi Colas and ate wedding cake while I drove.

We made it to the base with five minutes to spare.

After midnight I took June to an apartment I had rented a few weeks earlier. We were home at last, together, as husband and wife. Whew! What a trip! What a Christmas!

~ Gary L. Breezeel

The rest of the story…

Some years later we recognized the true nature of all that happened during those few days: my finding a ride to Dallas in answer to prayer, landing in Pittsburgh despite the snow, getting a marriage license without the required form, my family's seemingly impossible trek through a blizzard, my avoiding being AWOL by five minutes. Overcoming all these obstacles could only have been blessings from God.

Although the four days seemed like a comedy of errors, despite all the pitfalls and pratfalls, June and I got married at Christmas in 1969 and remain together after more than forty-four years.

~ 34 ~

Never an Angel

When I was a child, Christmas in the small logging town of Darrington, Washington, meant snow, carols, laughter, family, good things to eat, and multiple Christmas programs. The school and churches coordinated dates to avoid conflict. Most of the townsfolk traditionally attended as many programs as possible.

In those days before God got expelled from public schools, our combination elementary-high school, as well as the churches, included the Nativity in their annual programs. Shepherds, angels, and Wise Men contentedly rubbed elbows with toys, Santas, elves, snowmen, and snowflakes.

The year I was ten or eleven, the Methodist church had an all-girl angel choir. My heart raced when the white-robed figures with tinsel halos marched in carrying lighted candles and singing.

Would there ever be another such program? One where I could be an angel and wear a long, white robe and a tinsel halo?

Pageants came and went. Dozens of golden-haired angels announced the birth of Christ. I sadly watched the chosen ones proclaim, "Fear not…"

But never me! I was too tall, too scrawny, too plain. Years passed. Gray sprinkled my curly brown hair.

One particular Christmas after Mom and I moved to Auburn, Washington, I sat in a darkened church, reliving the Christmas story. Sadness that was all too familiar swept over me. I was too old to be an angel. Why couldn't I have been one of the pretty ones, one of those chosen? Didn't God think I was pretty or worthy enough?

Don't be stupid, I ordered myself. It isn't God who casts the pageants.

The thought didn't help. Neither did feeling guilty for thinking that way.

That Christmas my niece Julie was the beautiful, blonde angel who said, "Fear not…" She spoke her lines loud and clear, giving her best.

Suddenly it hit me!

Had I not done the same? Had I not given my best in every part I played? And in the pageant I had written? I thought of the joy I had experienced while retelling the age-old story in drama form. Of the thrill of becoming one of the shepherds in the fields, frightened by the great light, then filled with excitement when the angels came among us. The joyous proclamation rang in my ears: *"Fear not: for, behold, I bring you good tidings of great joy, which shall be to all people."* (Luke 2:10) I thought how my fellow shepherds and I had traveled to Bethlehem on that night of wonder.

My heart swelled when I pictured the Christ-child lying in the manger. What need had I to play the part of an angel? God had given me not what I longed for, but what He most needed from me. He gave me the ability to use my writing talent for him, to dramatize the story being enacted to the wonderment of those seeking to once more relive the true story of Christmas.

That Christmas, my bitterness slipped away, all traces of childhood rejection healed.

I've still never been an angel. Yet since my moment of realization during that Christmas program more than thirty years ago, I feel honored. God allowed me to repeat the words the Holy Angel said that first Christmas night…and allowed me to hear my niece recite them…

"Fear not…"

~ Colleen L. Reece

35

No Money, No Christmas

As the most special day of the year – besides my birthday – came closer, something happened that would change the way everyone in my family looked at Christmas for the rest of our lives. We still talk about it all these years later.

I grew up in a big family. We learned pretty early not to wait around for seconds at the dinner table. We also knew when it came to presents no one could ever expect to get everything on their list. But each Christmas we submitted lists to our parents anyway, hoping for something big that year.

This unforgettable Christmas happened over fifty years ago when I was just a boy. That special day was less than three weeks away, and the lists had already been handed in.

A special missionary speaker came to our church that December. He owned a big ship that took him to Eskimo villages. "Many of these people, especially the children, have nothing," he reported.

My parents often invited missionaries or special speakers to our home, so it wasn't out of the ordinary when they asked this Eskimos' missionary to our house for dinner. He told all sorts of wild stories about his ship, storms he had weathered, and the people he wanted to reach. "Their needs are great," he reminded our family later, "especially the children. Many of them will have nothing for Christmas."

Because I had so many brothers and sisters, my parents began saving Christmas money months in advance. Much of my father's income came from freelance writing, and a few books he had published.

I looked around to the large family sitting at our table. Our needs were pretty great too, I thought. Besides, Christmas was coming. I'd handed in my list, and now dreaming about what I'd get was all I could think about.

When it came to Christmas and presents, it's fair to say that I was, more or less, just as selfish as the next boy under ten years of age.

The missionary went on his way, and life returned to normal for the next few days…or so we thought.

Then, something more dramatic than any of my dad's stories happened. He called out in his loudest voice, "Family meeting! Family meeting!"

Anyone growing up in the Anderson house knew that "family meeting" always meant something big, really big, was about to happen. We had a family meeting when it was time to buy a new car, our first TV, when our father received a big royalty check, or we were going on vacation.

When we heard "family meeting" we nearly broke our necks running to the living room. Our big dog, Blitz, skidded around the corner, almost tripping me, just before I slid into my place on the floor wondering if this was the year I would finally get everything on my list. But then I noticed unusually serious looks on my parents' faces. Sometimes in family meetings they had to talk about difficult subjects. Those times were called family council.

"Mom and I have something important to discuss with you," our father began, "and your vote will help us decide what to do."

I swallowed hard, not sure I liked what my ears had just heard.

"You remember when the captain was here," he continued, "and told us about the needs in the Eskimo villages?"

I remembered worrying that I might have to give up something this year. My gaze darted around to my brothers and sisters. Most were staring down at the floor.

"Well," our mother added, "we were wondering if our family should do something to help."

"Like what?" my older sister asked.

My dad smiled. "We thought about taking the money we'd set aside for presents this year, and sending that to the captain for those children he told us about."

My chest tightened and I found it harder to breathe. My voice squeaked as I asked, "All of it?"

They nodded. I felt like one of my brothers had just kicked me in the stomach. My throat nearly squeezed shut, and a sick feeling took over my insides. This was Christmas. Our Christmas.

"So, what do you think?" my father asked.

I was pretty sure they didn't want to know what was really going through my head at that moment. I could imagine Eskimo children as presents were handed out. I envisioned a boy opening a present and it was exactly the same as the biggest gift I had written at the top of my list.

But my whole family began to talk about making Christmas better for others…together. And the missionary's words came back to my mind, "The needs are great. Many of the children will have nothing for Christmas."

Our family lived in Michigan where a white Christmas was never in doubt. The smell of this year's tree, already sitting over in the corner of the room where we would cast our votes, filled the air. It was beautifully decorated but had no presents under it yet.

No Christmas presents!

Then, one by one, hands began going up to vote yes on mailing our happy Christmas away to some Eskimo children we'd never meet. I could hardly believe it as I watched my own hand go up. The vote was unanimous.

It's fair to say that for the next few days, I was in a pretty bad mood. I didn't get along very well with my six brothers and sisters during that time.

Then, Christmas Eve day we again heard, "Family meeting!" That had never happened a second time so soon. When we raced to the living room this time, our parents had broad smiles on their faces.

"We have the most wonderful news," Dad told us. He held up an envelope. "I received a check in the mail today, for a story I had long forgotten about."

My mother's eyes glistened, her voice cracked with emotion as she said, "And it is exactly the same amount as we sent for the Eskimo children."

Well, I'm sure there has never been a more excited bunch of people before or since. Our parents rushed out to shop for Christmas. And they were gone for a long, long time.

Around the tree that night, our parents told us that because we were unselfish, and because they had to wait to shop the night before Christmas, everything was fifty percent off or more. Each of us got twice as much that year as any Christmas before.

And I'd thought there'd be no money for Christmas.

We all learned something special that year. Sometimes it's better to give…no matter what happens. Our money had blessed other kids living in desperate circumstances. In return, we were blessed beyond our young imaginations.

~ Max Elliot Anderson

❧ 36 ☙

Christmas 1952

The year was 1952. I was five years old. Sister Judy was twelve, brother Jim was eleven. Dad had not worked in months because of a herniated disc in his spine that caused immense pain and paralysis of his legs. Mom had begun working at the Union City Chair Factory upholstering the seats and backs of chrome kitchen chairs.

The winter was cold in our northeast corner of Pennsylvania. Each morning before going to school, my brother brought in coal to load the potbelly stove in the living room. It kept that room hot, the dining room and kitchen comfortable, the bedrooms and bath cool. Each morning, he pulled out the ash pan from the bottom of the stove and dumped it.

That morning Jim spilled the pan on the area rug that covered part of our living room floor. There were live coals among the ashes and Jim was stomping them out before a fire started but not before the rug was rife with burns.

My Dad, who was not tolerant of accidents, began yelling at my brother from his prone position on the couch. I stood there watching and wishing that I could help my brother. I knew my dad was hurting and I thought if the pain was eased he might not get so angry.

Our appetites for breakfast had been ruined by the incident that set Daddy off. Jim was sullen. Judy was attempting to become as invisible as possible. I sat there playing with my bowl of oatmeal. I didn't want to eat. Jim played with his toast. Judy twirled her long dark curls and looked at the clock. I knew she was asking God to move the hands on the clock faster so we could leave for school.

It was the last day before Christmas break. Tomorrow was Christmas Eve. I thought it would not be a happy Christmas.

That afternoon, after we returned from school and Mom came home from work, Jim brought in the hand-cut tree that he had dragged through the heavy snow from the woods to our home. He set the six-foot tree in the metal stand with the cut bottom of the trunk standing in a can of water. Mom draped the bottom with an old white sheet.

The four of us began to decorate while Dad lay on the couch, directing. "Jim, you put the lights on the tree."

"Yes, sir," Jim responded. He began the first string of lights at the bottom of the tree and draped the large colored lights over the branches as he walked around and around the tree.

Then Mom and Judy began to hang the ornaments. Some were very old and fragile glass, others were silver plastic and still others were homemade. They put a thin wire hook on the top of each bulb before hanging it carefully on the perfect branch. I was allowed to hang the plastic ornaments on the bottom branches. When the decoration boxes were empty Jim placed the silver star on the top of the tree. The last thing to hang were the silver icicles, hung one-by-one to make the tree glimmer. It looked like Christmas!

With the decorations complete it was time to drink our special treat: hot chocolate made with water and one large marshmallow slowly melting on top. It was an exciting time since we were anticipating that Santa would be arriving soon. I knew that if I wasn't asleep when Rudolph and Santa came to our home the sleigh would pass over and go to the next house, so I was eager to go to bed.

The next morning when I woke up I rushed out to see if Santa had stopped at our house. He had! I saw stockings lying on the white sheet under the tree, along with a few wrapped packages.

Mom kept me from running to the tree when she said we had to eat breakfast first.

I was so excited I could hardly swallow the soupy hot oatmeal with sugar and cinnamon. I thought the kitchen smelled like Christmas. Mom said it was the aroma of the stuffed turkey roasting in the oven, and a pumpkin pie that was baking.

With breakfast over it was time to open presents. At the living room door, Mom whispered something in Judy's ear. Judy whispered in Jim's ear. Jim whispered in my ear, "Don't forget its Dad's birthday today."

As soon as the words were out of Jim's mouth I squealed and ran over to

Dad. My intention was to wrap my arms around his neck, kiss his whiskered cheek and tell him, "Happy Birthday!"

"Don't jump on me," he said. His strong arms held me away.

Hurt, I bent my head and whispered, "I just wanted to wish you a happy birthday."

A flicker of remorse was in his eyes. "My back is hurting. But give me a kiss." He looked sad as he said, "It's a bad day of the year to have a birthday."

"No it's not Daddy," I said. "It's Baby Jesus' birthday. No one could have a more special birthday than that."

Dad cleared his throat, looked at Mom and said, "It must be time for the kids to open their socks."

Holding my sock, I pulled out first an orange, next came an apple and then a beautiful red and white striped candy cane wrapped in cellophane. In the very bottom of the toe were a walnut, an almond and a Brazil nut still in their shells. I turned the sock upside down and shook it to make sure there wasn't something else. Nothing came out. Judy and Jim's socks were duplicates of mine.

Mom handed a present to Judy. It was a used book. Judy exclaimed that it was exactly what she had hoped for. Mom handed a present to Jim. As he took off the wrapping paper I could see that Santa had brought him a pair of black, high top sneakers. They looked pretty neat but the bottoms looked a little worn. Santa must be having as difficult a year as we were.

Mom handed me a package wrapped in green paper. Inside was a grey stuffed lamb. It was beautiful. Next came a red package; inside was a black stuffed cat. The lamb and the cat were made of material that was shiny and slippery but they were soft and I loved them. This was a very special Christmas.

I was careful not to jump on Daddy but I went over and kissed his cheek while everyone else was cleaning up the paper and putting the living room back in order. I noticed that he and Mom didn't get any presents under the tree. I wondered if they hadn't been good all year but then I reasoned that they must have been or they would have gotten a piece of coal.

Dad stumbled in pain to the dinner table and offered a prayer of thanks to God for his son, the baby Jesus. We celebrated Dad's birthday by singing the birthday song, and with a candle in the center of the pumpkin pie. I thought we were having a wonderful Christmas while my family shared the meal and celebrated two special birthdays.

While Judy and Jim were doing the dishes together, I took my new animals into the bedroom Judy and I shared, and lay on our bed playing with them. Once the clatter of dishes stopped, all was quiet and little sounds floated through our small house.

I could hear Christmas music coming from our record player. My head moved from shoulder to shoulder as I hummed along with "Have Yourself a Merry Little Christmas."

Thinking back on that Christmas, I now realize it was, in many ways, our most difficult one. In another way it was perhaps the most blessed.

Christmas is not just about the gifts, food, decorations or even whether a family member is critical or encouraging. Christmas is about loving one another in all circumstances, being together as a family, and celebrating our Savior's birth.

~ *Toni Armstrong Sample*

The rest of the story…

Years late, I learned that Mom had made my two special toys that year. She used discarded pieces of plastic material and padding that were left over from the upholstery she worked with at the factory. She visited the Salvation Army thrift store for Judy's book and Jim's boots. With Dad being unable to work, she did the best she could to give us a memorable Christmas.

We are all the product of our childhood – some wonderful moments and some not so wonderful. It is truly how God leads us to use those experiences in our life that matters.

I am so very grateful that I was raised by a woman of faith who brought her children up in the church.

My Mom is ninety-five now, but in good mental and physical health. She's a small but mighty powerhouse, and my best friend. It has been an amazing experience to write about my childhood and share the stories with my mom. They have helped her with her memory and are a continuing part of the special journey that she and I continue to share.

ns 37 ~

Meeting Jesus at the Toilet Bowl

For some, the Christmas season arrives the day after Thanksgiving when the beautifully carved Nativity scene and brightly colored ornaments are unloaded from the attic. For others, the celebration of our Savior's birth begins with the first exchange of gifts. For me, Christmas is heralded on December twenty-fourth when the first four notes of "Joy to the World" are played on the chancel organ.

One year, my anticipation rose to an all-time high. Every member of our family was scheduled, in one capacity or another, to help during the Christmas Eve worship service. Despite being a bit puny from a nasty stomach virus two days earlier, our youngest son promised to be an adorable but dignified little torchbearer who would light the Advent wreath.

Scheduled to be the crucifer, our middle son would carry the large gold cross and lead the entire procession from the narthex into the church sanctuary. Our sixteen-year-old would assist the minister in preparing the wine for communion. My husband and I would be in the choir loft, joining our voices in Handel's "Hallelujah Chorus."

Throughout the entire month of December, I not only envisioned the perfect Christmas celebration, I relished it. My tears were a wellspring of pride and joy.

I was also frenzied with activity. I poured over an extensive To Do list, checking off each agenda item successfully completed.

Decorate the church's fellowship hall for Baby Jesus' birthday party. Check.

Make two more batches of chocolate fudge and four dozen sugar cookies for members of the congregation who do not want birthday cake. Check.

Wrap gifts for Secret Prayer Pals. Not checked.

Practice "Hallelujah Chorus." Not checked.

The list seemed endless. By the time I had less than twenty-four hours left, I noticed a growing queasiness in my stomach but passed it off as exhaustion or excitement or a combination of both. I adore sweets, so it was also reasonable to assume that I had eaten too many homemade goodies from the office.

By midnight, though, I faced the grim reality that my ever-increasing nausea wasn't exhaustion, excitement, or too much chocolate fudge. I had a stomach virus. I was on my first round of vomiting and diarrhea when our oldest son hollered from the upstairs bathroom. Within the hour, my husband had also fallen victim to this vicious viral attack.

Lying on the bathroom floor during the wee hours of the morning, I began to think about Jesus' mother as she journeyed on the back of a donkey, laboring with her firstborn child. Did she experience the nausea I experienced while in labor with our third son? Was the back pain severe as she swayed side to side, balancing upon the back of an unwieldy beast?

As I gripped the edge of the toilet bowl, my thoughts shifted to the perfect Christmas Eve I had envisioned only hours earlier. The trays of sweets, lovingly prepared by my own hands the previous day as a gift for the congregation, would be thrown into the garbage can at the side of the house.

My secret prayer pal would go home without a gift under the tree, wondering about my identity, wondering if she had been accidentally forgotten. The "Hallelujah Chorus" would be sung without my husband's strong tenor voice in the choir loft. Our sons' responsibilities would be fulfilled by other mothers' children.

The only tears that I would cry that day would be tears of nausea and pain, tears of unfulfilled expectations, tears of self pity.

Then, I realized the truth. I would not hear our organist play the first notes of "Joy to the World." But Christmas would come!

Christmas would come, because a brave young woman – despite her fears of pain or tears of unfulfilled expectations – gave birth to the Son of God in a lowly stable on the outskirts of Bethlehem.

God didn't need my frenzied activity leading up to the twenty-fourth of December, my dedication to tradition, my cookies, or my fudge. He didn't need our voices in the choir singing "Joy to the World" or the "Hallelujah Chorus." He didn't need our stately red robes or beautifully wrapped secret pal gifts. And he definitely didn't need me to deliver Christmas. Christmas would come because of our Father's immeasurable love for each and everyone of us, and it would be perfect.

As I lay on the bathroom floor, my thoughts drifted to the shame-filled Samaritan woman who encountered Jesus on the outskirts of Sychar. A well or a toilet bowl, it really didn't matter. Our stories were very much the same. Relationships with men too numerous to count filled the Samaritan woman with guilt and shame, while church activities too numerous to count puffed me up with sinful pride. Both of us encountered the Lord at a low point in our lives…not because we went looking for Him but because He came looking for us.

We offered him nothing. But He offered us grace, and gratefully we received.

~ *Sherry Schumann*

Dear Lord Jesus,
Thank you for creatively planning encounters to address those issues which interfere in my relationship with you. Who else but you would have thought of meeting me at a toilet bowl?
Love, Sherry

~ 38 ~

Christmas Watercolor

I had my suitcase packed and ready. The intense heat of summer in Central Florida lingered into fall. I looked forward to our yearly autumn retreat in Asheville, North Carolina, to usher in the holiday season. "This is just what I need," I reasoned with my husband. "It's been a while since we've gone to the mountains. They say it's good for the soul."

"Do they have businesses to run?"

"It's a God thing, Dennis."

He laughed. "Going to the mountains is God's business?"

"Yep. I think he does some of his best work at higher altitudes."

"I won't argue with that. I only hope he helps me figure out a way to pay for this trip."

"He will," I said, and smiled as we got into the car before sunrise.

By mid-afternoon we zipped along the Blue Ridge Parkway as it climbed high into the misty clouds, winding ever upward. "It's like a spiral stairway to heaven," I said, and soon I was rocked into a state of euphoria. One by one, all my worries floated away like leaves drifting in the wind. Autumn's harvest reminded me of the songs God planted in me, the abundant love he has for all who seek to see him, and this undeniable calling to the mountains that took root in my heart when I was a child.

My mind wandered to reflect on a list of events of years past – the births of my sons, family vacations, weddings, skiing, snowball fights, snowmen that resembled the Liberty Bell, and the holidays – Christmas, my favorite time of year.

And then without warning, my eyes welled with tears.

I thought about all the loved ones who were no longer with us for the holidays. I closed my eyes and thought of my parents whom I miss the most. I remember the sound as I padded down the hallway in my new flannel, footy pajamas on Christmas Eve when I was a child living in New York City.

My sister and I would slide across our parquet wood floors and pretend we were ice-skating at Rockefeller Center, or across a frozen lake. I could almost smell my mother's Christmas cookies and see the sparkling ornaments on our stylish silver aluminum foil tree.

We drank hot chocolate. We ate cherry gumdrops. I dreamed candy cane dreams. Santa's gifts made me smile until my cheeks hurt – especially Raggedy Ann and Andy, Barbie, Ken, and my favorite huge dolly, named Giggles. She became my best friend, and she even let me cut her hair. Giggles also let my dad screw bolts into her neck to keep her head on her shoulders after I threw her across the room a few years later. She didn't mind if she looked like Herman Munster – even if I did.

I also remembered the free Ronald McDonald stuffed doll my mom liked. She'd say, "He has red hair just like you."

I would look at her and say, "He has red hair like you."

The memory of loss took over again. My mind focused on a neglected patch of weeds at home in Florida that had become a beautiful garden where we buried our Golden Retriever. She sleeps among the speckled tiger lilies that resemble my mother's orange high-heeled sandals. Now as I looked out at the mountain scenery, through my tears I thought of the falling leaves that resembled the copper-colored hair of our retriever and my mom.

Wiping my tears away, I focused on the beauty around me. As my eyes traced the colorful tapestry formed by nature, I realized that crooked branches, uneven ridges, and dark crags are a part of God's big picture. The lower elevation trees were wearing a golden crown; I wondered why I seldom thanked the one who crowned them. I let all the nuances of autumn soak into my soul as I looked at how God transformed the formerly all green landscape and places we might call imperfections into a magnificent watercolor painting.

As we drove higher, my gaze lifted to the highest points of the mountains, dotted with brilliant red leaves. It was as if God had decorated his mountain the way I would decorate one tree with red balls or bows.

A sudden gust of wind reminded me that winter was right around the corner. That would usher in Christmas.

My soul sings in anticipation and longs to focus on the wonder, not the chaos, the season brings. And I'll admit, for me part of the wonder begins the moment I convince my husband to buy the tallest live tree we can find in Florida. "It reminds me of the mountains," I'll say in a pouty voice.

    He tries to reason. "The tree won't fit through the door."

    Yet we always wind up with a humongous twelve-to-fourteen footer.

    I want to cling to all the sweet moments God has given me, as if they are all pieces of a priceless watercolor painting. All are gifts. None are wrapped in expensive paper. They can't fit under the tallest hemlock, spruce, or majestic fir.

    Some are new beginnings…another opportunity for us to mourn, forgive, let go, or give of ourselves. Our children, friends, and our pets, all deck our halls with boughs of love – if only for a season. And I know that unlike most paintings these gifts are wrapped in ribbons of love's purest whites and fiery reds, and banana yellow bows that look like smiles. But, they are tied together with strands of deep grays, and blue sorrows.

    They are all my miracles, and broken dreams. My successes. My failures.

    This is the true rendition of my life – my Christmas Watercolor.

    So, this Christmas I will hang two wooden doves from a very rustic ten-foot tree – nah, maybe twelve. One dove will represent all my prayers…even the ones that haven't been answered the way I asked. The other represents the gifts that adorn my life. Faith. Hope. Peace. And love.

~ Joann M. Claypoole

❧ 39 ❧

Having a Blue, Blue Christmas

"I think we should cancel Christmas this year," I told my husband.

He sighed. "Maybe you're right."

Financial pressures and the disappointment of having no children home for Christmas had dampened my spirits. Battling the flu for several weeks accompanied by many sleepless nights had lulled me into a somberness of soul.

I thumbed through the address book and wrote out a few cards, finding no energy to even sign my name. How could I honestly wish my friends a blessed season when I wished Christmas would never come?

We'd decided on money gifts that year since our grown children seemed to have everything they wanted that was within our financial reach. As I sealed the envelopes, my eyes filled with tears. I yearned for Christmases of long ago when the house bustled with excitement, a time when I woke with tired eyes to the wonder that children bring to Christmas morning.

I missed last minute shopping, scotch tape and glitter carpeting the floor, and frantic searches for lost shears. I missed pulling my hair out trying to shuffle seven courses on a four-burner stovetop.

It wouldn't seem like Christmas unless I felt frenzied.

Christmas had always been my favorite holiday. I planned for it all year. I loved the smell of cinnamon bread, cranberry gelatin, pumpkin pie, and gingerbread cookies. I loved keeping a supply of candy and nuts, and feasting at all hours of the day. I loved waiting for the kids to fall asleep so I could sneak downstairs to fill stockings full of gum and trinkets. I loved being awakened soon after by exuberant gift seekers anxious to open presents. I'd laugh as I hurdled my way through the living room over mounds of torn wrapping and strewn treasures to get another cup of freshly brewed coffee.

Unfortunately, the seasons of our lives are never stagnant. Change inevitably creeps and twines its way, strangling cherished traditions.

The worst consequence of the empty nest syndrome was Christmas without the children. All three lived out of state.

Employment demands, conflicting needs of in-laws, and the miles between us prevented celebrating many holidays together. Visits were grabbed like inexpensive hotel rooms – at the convenience of off-season rates.

More out of habit than desire, I dragged out the ornament box. We'd long since reduced the real eight-foot-tree to an artificial four-foot one on a table. I missed the smell of fresh pine and a tree and presents taking up half the living room.

I was facing another uneventful Christmas, all too quiet and trimmed down. I sighed as I rummaged through the depleting assortment of decorations and picked up a small fabric angel.

As I displayed it prominently on a small branch, I thought of angels hovering near the Christ Child. Assembling the Nativity set, I saw a small tiny baby born in a cold barn, His bed made from a feeding bin and filled with prickly straw. His layette was a burial cloth, a symbol of the very reason He came. I saw shepherds kneeling to a Baby King born into poverty.

It was a strange way to send the Messiah.

As I emptied myself of the disappointments that choked my joy, I focused on The Child, and my spirit sprang to new life. I stopped focusing on what I missed and thought of what I have – precious memories. And now my grown children were making memories of their own, taking the good of their youth and adding to the joys of their own families.

Most of all, I thanked God for the gift of himself – a gift independent of wealth, status, and circumstances, or even an empty nest – God who sacrificed his only Son so that I can spend eternity with him.

As I set the Nativity in place, I looked at my husband. He sighed, then grinned, and winked at me as if he'd been waiting for me to realize what I have...including him.

"Merry Christmas," he said.

~ Linda Wood Rondeau

∽ 40 ∾

A Is the Answer

My dream was to write inspirational fiction, preferably suspenseful stories that intrigue, yet encourage the reader's relationship with God. When I started writing my first novel I became bogged down in the middle of an outline that meandered like an endless lazy river with no destination, or a maze with no beginning and no end.

Discouraged, I would put the outline aside and fall back to writing "by the seat of my pants," meaning I would write whatever came to mind with no formal direction. That didn't work either. I wrote my novel into a plot hole.

Official definition of a plot hole? A gap that defies logic.

My definition? Frustration.

I was alone in my efforts as a beginning novelist because I didn't know anyone to consult who had expertise in the field. Discouraged and feeling inept, I began to pray. As I did, the Bible verse John 15:5 came to mind. *"I am the vine; you are the branches. He who abides in Me, and I in him bears much fruit; for without Me you can do nothing."*

I was not alone. I was just trying to go it alone, so I prayed, "Father, if it is your desire for me to write for your glory, please guide me and connect me with the right people."

Afterwards I felt led to perform an online search for guidance on writing outlines for novels. That guided me to an organization's website whose national writer's conference was coming up soon in Denver, Colorado. My search yielded a session titled, "How to Outline Your Novel with an EXCEL Spreadsheet."

Intrigued, I clicked on the link. As an accountant I work with spreadsheets daily, but couldn't fathom how a writer could outline a novel with one. The session description convinced me that it was exactly what I needed. The problem was that I live in South Carolina. A plane ticket – in addition to the cost of conference registration and hotel – was not an option.

As disappointment settled over me because I could not attend, I clicked on the speaker's bio, then her website. I was delighted to learn that she wrote in the romantic suspense genre.

I was equally stunned when I clicked on her events page and saw that her next speaking engagement was the upcoming weekend…only thirty minutes from my home. In awe, I read that she would be teaching the same class as the one in Denver, and if that wasn't enough, she lived about an hour from me.

Excited, I checked out the website for the South Carolina conference. I registered, along with a friend, who although she was not a writer, daily encouraged me to write. Three days later I was immersed in a world of writing, editing, and publishing that I hadn't known existed so close to my home.

The author's method of using the spreadsheet to organize the entire novel resonated with me, and helped plug up the plot holes in my novel. The fact that she was in the right place at the right time in my life steered me to other writers in her circle, which led to my first short story being published.

It also resulted in an invitation to a Christmas luncheon with new writer friends at The Cove, Billy Graham's Christian conference center, where afterwards we retreated to a private room to fellowship and exchange Christmas gifts. Each writer had been instructed to bring a gift that begins with the letter "A."

Most of the women in the group had known each other for a while and most were accomplished, published authors, but the warmth of these women who shared my passion of writing soon put me at ease.

We sat in a circle and waited for each woman to open her surprise gift. When it was my turn, I pulled the brightly colored tissue from the bag and lifted out a shiny letter "A" paperweight with a picture holder at the top. The accompanying Christmas card said, "Choose a goal or a project that you would like to Accomplish in 2014 and I will be your Accountability partner! Merry Christmas, Lori."

I immediately thought of my earlier prayer for God to send help and connect me with the right people. My plea had initiated a never ending string of answers, from a cure for an ailing outline and failing novel to a year's worth of support from a published author.

As I absorbed the beauty of the Cove in all its Christmas finery, I marveled at how God made possible what seemed impossible, how he used an aimless novel outline to lead me to my destiny. And how he used a simple Christmas gift of the letter "A" to offer me complete Affirmation.

~ *Fran Lee Strickland*

❧ 41 ❧

The Gift of a Lifetime

I hurried through the crowded mall, searching for last-minute Christmas gifts for my husband and children. For several years, my holiday shopping also included gifts my elderly parents wanted me to buy for their large family of married children and grandchildren.

This meant their gift to me was never a surprise, because I always bought it!

But this Christmas was different. My parents didn't mention gifts or ask me to shop for them. I didn't mind, having plenty of shopping of my own to do. But as I dodged shoppers in the store aisles, I wondered – were my parents too old to care about gift giving? After all, both were in their eighties, and Father was nearing ninety.

On Christmas Eve, my husband and I picked up my parents at their apartment to drive them to the family celebration. To my surprise, they greeted us with faces wreathed in smiles, and arms loaded with various-shaped Christmas presents. "Our gifts for the family came, and we just finished wrapping them," Mom said, excitement in her voice.

Dad and Mom chattered happily in the backseat of our station wagon during the half-hour drive to my sister's home. Sometimes they whispered to each other in German, obviously pleased with their secret. Dying of curiosity, I asked, "So what did you get me for Christmas?" They chuckled but didn't reply.

"How about a little hint?" But I couldn't coax a single clue out of them.

When we arrived at my sister's home, the sage-laced aroma of roast turkey welcomed us along with hugs and cheerful greetings of, "Merry Christmas!" and "Good to see you!" We shed our coats and gathered near the crackling fireplace, chatting as background music proclaimed, "Joy to the world, the Lord is come!"

After feasting on turkey and all the trimmings, we settled around the twinkling, tinseled tree. As usual, Dad read the Christmas story aloud from the Bible. He seemed hurried, and didn't comment much on the passage.

Then it was time to exchange gifts. Dad spoke up. "Mom and I want to be the first to give our gifts, but don't open them until everyone has one." He read the names from each package as Mom handed them to the children and grandchildren.

Two generations waited in suspense, curious about the contents of the boxes. When we all had our presents, Dad said, "Now you may open them."

Sounds of tearing paper filled the room, followed by several of us asking, "What's this?" as assorted food boxes emerged beneath the wrappings. Surely the gifts couldn't be what the cartons said. We opened Shredded Wheat and Hi Ho Crackers boxes, but we did not find cereal or crackers.

We each discovered the same gift – a book.

As we held our books, my white-haired father spoke in a quavering voice. "As I approach my ninetieth birthday, I have a strong desire to leave something behind to speak when I can't."

The thought of Dad dying added a somber quietness to the moment.

He glanced at Mom, who nodded and patted his leg in encouragement. "As I looked back on the exciting and touching experiences in our lives, I felt a deep yearning to share them with others."

I glanced down at my book, *Heartcries and Blessings: The Reflections of a Russian-born Servant of God* by Nicolai Siemens. It held stories written by my father, whose German ancestors had settled in Russia at the invitation of Catherine the Great.

I recalled stories he had told me of his life — stories of religious persecution, imprisonment in Russia as a Mennonite minister, God's intervention, and their miraculous escape in 1929.

Dad continued. "I began to pray like Job, 'Oh that my words were printed in a book!'" (Job 19:23) The printing of this book is an answer to many, many prayers." He pulled out a handkerchief and wiped his tears.

The room was silent. Completely surprised, none of us knew how to respond. We looked at our books, each one carefully inscribed with a personal message. Mine read: "Lydia, your artistic talents are paying dividends at home and in the church. We love you. Your parents, Nicolai and Helen Siemens."

I glanced through the pages and saw personal stories, poems, and spiritual insights. I began reading, only half registering the recorded memories.

I was too stunned to fully appreciate their gift that Christmas. At that time, my parents were alive, sitting near me, and I could talk to them in person. But two years later, they both passed away, and then I realized how priceless their gift was.

Now, decades later, with grown children and grandchildren of my own, I treasure my surprise gift far more than I thought possible. I'm inspired by my father's courage to self-publish a book at age eighty-nine. Because Dad took the time to record these stories, my family and generations yet unborn can learn about their Christian heritage. His testimony echoes the Psalmist's words: *They will still bear fruit in old age, they will stay fresh and green, proclaiming, "The Lord is upright; he is my Rock."* (Psalm 92:14–15 NIV)

My parents weren't too old to care about gift giving. Instead, they gave a priceless gift – one that outlasted any others.

A righteous man will be remembered forever.
Psalm 112:6 (NIV)

~ *Lydia E. Harris*

❧ 42 ❧
The Spirit of Christmas

One of my favorite Christmas songs is "That Spirit of Christmas," performed by Ray Charles. It's about a kind of Christmas spirit that doesn't depend on circumstances, and endures beyond December. When I was a child, I thought Christmas spirit meant decorating, listening to carols, exchanging presents and being with family. I think back to a time when I couldn't wait to get up in the morning, hoping for a new bicycle. I still remember the feeling of anticipation.

As I got older, I recognized that cookies, gifts, and holiday traditions were blessings. But why, I wondered, couldn't that spirit of Christmas remain all through the year?

Then, as I grew into adulthood, I was confronted with an unsettling reality: How can we experience the Christmas spirit during the holiday even when we suffer the loss of a job or a loved one, or a terminal illness? How can we find comfort and joy, hope and peace, when our todays and our yesterdays are painful, and our tomorrows look even worse?

As I matured and studied, the connection between the virgin birth, the Holy Spirit, and my ability to live with Christmas spirit year round became a life-changing revelation for me. I found an anchor that could not be moved by despair, dread, disease, or even death. I discovered the most wonderful book ever written. From cover to cover, the Bible is filled with Christmas memories.

I had heard critics say Matthew didn't believe the virgin birth, that he was just quoting Isaiah, and Isaiah's word for virgin just means "female teenager." I wondered what Matthew really believed, after living with Jesus for three years.

It struck me that Matthew would have been very wealthy if he had remained in his job as tax collector. Luke gives us two words that Matthew was too modest to record about what it cost Matthew to follow Jesus: He "left everything." (Luke 5:28) Matthew was willing to do what the rich young ruler would not. I could see that something extremely persuasive motivated Matthew.

One day as I was reading the Christmas story, I discovered what Matthew really believed about the virgin birth. The book of Luke lists the ancestors of Mary, while Matthew gives Joseph's family tree. Matthew wrote: Jacob fathered Joseph the husband of Mary, from whom was born Jesus who is called the Messiah. (Matthew 1:16)

In its original language, Matthew's word translated "whom" is very specific. It's singular feminine. Matthew, who was listing Joseph's genealogy, wrote that Jesus was born of Mary only, not Mary and Joseph.

These genealogies came to life for me because I am part of the same family – God's family. The list of names reminds me that God is faithful to keep His promises, from generation to generation.

Two of the happiest events in my family are weddings and births. I think of Jesus' genealogy as a fireworks display – wedding-birth-wedding-birth. Like an Olympic highlights video, these are the "Kodak moments" over hundreds of years. Whenever I read the list of names, I hear a drum roll leading up to the glorious grand finale: the virgin birth of Christ.

I recognized many years ago that gifts and cookies and holiday traditions are blessings, but the greatest blessing is the true Spirit of Christmas. The Spirit of Christmas is the Spirit of God, who conceived the Son of God, whose birth we celebrate.

The same Holy Spirit who enabled the birth of Christ and the birth of the church indwells every true believer. Because He will never leave me, I have comfort and joy, hope and peace, the true Spirit of Christmas all through the year, and for eternity.

At the first Christmas, God came to us in Christ. Because Christ came to us, I can come to God, with the comfort that my sins are forgiven. That is the best Christmas gift I have ever received, or ever will – far better than the bicycle which once meant so much to me.

With every gift under the tree and every holiday tradition, anticipation builds before the event, then it's over. But when I received the gift of the true Spirit of Christmas, my anticipation grew after the gift.

It's still growing.

- John Kincaid

43

Christmas Lights

In the pre-dawn darkness, I turned on the colored lights of my three Christmas trees, the green and white lights on the garland gracing the stair railing and loft ledge, and the row of clear icicle lights on the front porch, intending to let them shine all Christmas day. I said "Happy Birthday" to Jesus as I turned them on.

Well, then he turned on his own light. The sun began to shine across the sky and all over the landscape, and my little lights faded. The huge lights on the tall magnolia across the street lost their brilliance. One would have to look closely to see any lights at all.

In my office, the lights on my two-foot tree became little colored dots…if I looked closely. What I saw instead were plastic limbs and twisted green wires that looked like a jumbled mess. Some of the little "gold" balls were missing from the string of garland, some with the coating scratched off were looped unevenly.

What looks pretty in the dark becomes a jumbled mess when exposed to God's light. It made me think that no matter what we do, what we accomplish, our best is no more than fake – a muddle that means little unless the light of Jesus shines through us. We can still give out a little light on our own, do some good, but we can never do our best without the light of Jesus in our hearts.

Unless we're plugged in to him and his light is shining through us, we will be like a jumbled mess existing in darkness. It's so true that Jesus said, "I am the light of the world," and "you are the light of the world."

On my own I might occasionally be able to shine like a little dot of light. But I would rather make sure it's his light that shines through me.

- Yvonne Lehman

44

Remembering Christmas

Tears streamed down my cheeks as I stood by the chain-link fence and watched the Mission Aviation Fellowship (MAF) plane take off from Zambuanga without me. It was December 23rd. The plane was headed home for the Christmas holidays, and I'd been left behind.

Uncle Jim let me watch until the plane was out of sight before we headed back to the guesthouse. The trip was made in silence. My emotions were too overwhelming to say anything and Uncle Jim respected my inability to speak. On our way, I pondered the events of the previous twenty-four hours.

On December 22nd, I had been at boarding school at Faith Academy in Manila, Philippines. Dad and Mom were missionaries, and home for me was the island of Irian Jaya, Indonesia. I hadn't been home since school started the first week in August. That morning, I boarded the Philippine airliner excitedly. There were eight of us in the group: my brother, Danny, and sister, Becci, and several friends who also lived in Irian Jaya. We were bound for Zambuanga, the southernmost island in the Philippines. On the ground, MAF pilot, Uncle Clell, had greeted us along with Uncle Jim, the host of the guesthouse where we would be staying.

After supper, Uncle Clell was checking all the paperwork required for immigration, when he called me into the dining room. "Sharon, your Indonesian Residency Papers are missing and there is no visa to enter Indonesia stamped in your passport yet!"

I just stood, stunned. How could my Residency Papers and visa have been overlooked? Without them, I would not be able to go home for Christmas.

"There is an embassy on the island of Mindinao," Uncle Clell continued. I began to get my hopes up. Maybe I could still go home. But I didn't like the hesitation in his voice.

"However, if you flew there tomorrow to get your visa, we wouldn't be able to fly to Indonesia until Christmas day. The Lunow and Preston kids wouldn't get home until the day after Christmas."

The other kids had gathered around us by this time, sensing that something was wrong. I felt dizzy. Everyone else's fate depended on the decision I had to make: Go get the visa and have everyone else home late for Christmas, or stay behind. I did not like my options. I knew it would be selfish to get the visa, but where would I go if I stayed behind? I knew no one on the island of Zambuanga, and I did not want to go back to Manila.

"I guess I'll have to stay behind," I stammered.

I felt the tears forming, and I didn't want to be seen crying, so I went to the room where I was spending the night. I crawled into bed and sobbed into the pillow. I pleaded, "Dear God, I don't want to go back to Manila. The dorms have closed for Christmas break, and I don't want to try and find a place to stay there. I feel so lost!"

When I finally stopped crying, I dug out the Christmas presents for my family from my suitcase, and gave them to Becci. In shock, I listlessly watched a couple of my friends playing ping-pong in the rec-room.

"Sharon." I started as my name was spoken. I had not seen Uncle Clell enter the room.

"Uncle Jim was just talking with me. He and Aunt Nancy have a daughter, Carrie, who is a senior this year, so she is just two years older than you are. Her brother, Justin, is a junior. You have been invited to spend Christmas with them."

I could hardly believe what I was hearing. I wouldn't be able to go home, but neither did I have to go back to Manila. God had answered my prayer! I gratefully accepted the invitation.

When Uncle Jim and I arrived back at the guesthouse, Carrie helped me take my luggage to her room and unpack. It was midmorning, and I hadn't been able to eat any breakfast. Carrie led me to the kitchen where she showed me how to make eggnog. She poured a glass of milk about three-quarters full, so there would be room for an egg, a tablespoon of sugar and a dash of nutmeg. This was whisked together. Mom always made eggnog for me when I was sick, so I found the drink very comforting.

Carrie helped make my stay in Zambuanga a time of confusing delight.

We played my favorite sport, soccer, with other missionary children in the neighborhood during the afternoons. At first these games made me homesick, longing to be with my family and friends. In the evenings we put puzzles together and played games. My stomach sometimes knotted up as I thought about how I would be putting puzzles together with Mom or playing marbles with Dad if I were home.

Carrie also took me shopping, and I was able to purchase gifts for this family who had so graciously invited me into their home. She gave me a tour of Zambuanga and shared her favorite hangouts with me.

Christmas day arrived, and to my surprise, I found a pink stocking with my name on it underneath the Christmas tree! Aunt Nancy had made it for me. It held a pair of earrings with anchors on them; a pretty shell to add to my collection; and a Philippine dancing doll. The anchor earrings were especially precious to me because they reminded me that God is the anchor of my faith, and that no storm would ever overtake me where He was not in full control.

After gifts were exchanged, I went back to the room I shared with Carrie, and read again the Christmas story from the second chapter of the Gospel of Luke. Verse seven held special meaning for me: [Mary] gave birth to her firstborn, a son. She wrapped him in cloths and put him in a manger, because there was no room for them in the inn.

Jesus wasn't home in heaven that first Christmas day either! He left heaven to become the God-man, who would die on the cross for my sins.

It was that Christmas when I came to appreciate, in a new way, how much Jesus loved me. Jesus also showed His love to me through this loving family who opened their home to me and helped me celebrate his birthday in a way I would forever remember.

~ *Sharon J. Morris*

❧ 45 ❦

Home for Christmas

Bing Crosby's mellow voice floated through our home that December long ago, melodiously promising, "I'll be home for Christmas…"

"Daddy is 'home for Christmas.'" Mother spoke softly through her tears to my younger brother, eleven-year-old Frank, and my nine-year-old sister, Dotty. They sat below me on the front hall stairs of our old family farmhouse in Maine.

I slid down a step and ran my fingers through my mother's chestnut hair, streaked with silver. "That's not quite what we had in mind when we prayed that Dad would be home from the hospital for Christmas," I told her.

Thinking of the unexpected tragedy that had begun our day, I peered past my father's car in the drive outside to the frozen fields and forest beyond. In the living room I could see the lights twinkle on the Christmas tree, waiting for Dad's return.

"Your father is with Jesus," Mother answered me simply. "I couldn't wish him back. He's happy where he is." Mother, though in grief, answered with calm assurance. She and Dad had walked together with the Lord for nearly three decades. But her voice gave no hint of the shock at having Dad taken home by the Lord just before the celebration of the greatest birth ever known.

The small children's wondering faces pressed close to our mother's wool coat while she hugged them together. As I watched, I thought of my own child, a two-year-old daughter in the apartment above, now being comforted by my pregnant wife, Dot.

The next evening our little Debbie warmed adult hearts with her intuitive, "Grandpa's sleeping," as he lay in his casket.

Christmas, I learned that season, is a celebration of both birth and death. Mary wept for joy at the birth of her Babe. The Bible also records that Rachel, symbolic of all mothers in Israel, wept in grief at Christmastime. (Jeremiah 31:15) Her babe was slain by Roman soldiers at the command of

Herod, fearful that the Christ child would replace him as king. (Matthew 2:16-18)

Whether death comes in peace and fullness of years, or by violence in youth, it is no less final, no less tragic. Only in accepting death as God's will and looking to his provision, which began with that birth in Bethlehem, can any death have meaning.

Some may find it strange to think about death at Christmastime. But the simple fact is, Jesus was born in the manger long ago precisely because a loving God saw that the world is dying. In the best-known words of Jesus, speaking of both his own birth and his death, he said, *"God so loved the world that he gave his only begotten Son, that whoever believes in Him shall not perish but have everlasting life."* (John 3:16 NASB) The death of a loved one at Christmas only underscores why Jesus came to the manger and to Mary's arms.

A generation after the Romans killed the male babies of Bethlehem, another Herod assented to Christ's death. A second troop of Roman soldiers put to death the One who had been hunted by the elder Herod. And Mary, like Rachel, wept.

The person who both Herods wanted killed was, and is, the King of kings.

The sad truth is that we, too, are guilty of his blood. But through his death, if we believe and repent, we have forgiveness of all our sins. (Romans 4:24-25; 5:1) Yet the good news is that God did not send his Son into the world to condemn the world, but that whoever believes in him should not be condemned with the unbelievers, but be set free from his or her sins and saved from God's judgment. (John 3:17–18)

This is the crux of the story: Christ was born on Christmas Day. He was born that no more Rachels need weep.

Jesus stood one day before a tomb and told two grieving sisters, *"Whoever lives and believes in me shall never die."* (John 11:26) This was his promise that those who believe in him will never have to face eternal death.

The familiar song Bing Crosby sang tells of being home for Christmas, if only in the heart. For a truly joyous celebration, the heart must harbor both the cradle and the cross.

Paul summed it up this way: If you confess with your mouth the Lord Jesus, and believe in your heart that God has raised him from the dead, you will be saved. (Romans 10:9) Our real home, at Christmas or any day of the year, is by faith with Jesus in God's family.

- Eric E. Wiggin

The rest of the story...

I'll Be Home for Christmas....
I listened to Luciano Pavarotti sing this song one recent Christmas Eve. I cried. I couldn't help it. Yet I had great joy in this experience. My brother Frank, for a time responsible for security oversight in a federally contracted munitions plant, found that someone had posted my *Power for Living* story about our dad's untimely death on the bulletin board of the factory's break room. Frank was quite excited when he phoned me with "Junior, I saw your story!"

The first time I remember hearing the song was the year Dad died...and was home for Christmas.

❧ 46 ❦
A Season of Joy

No colorful lights outlined the roof of the old, white frame house that served as a shelter to the homeless. No Christmas tree sat at the front window showing off twinkling lights to passers-by. The curtain was drawn, and the house sat in darkness.

I pulled around back to the office, turned off my car, and sat gazing at the house that reflected my own level of holiday cheer. Because of a broken marriage, for the first time ever my family wouldn't be celebrating Christmas together. And I was supposed to talk about joy tonight. I opened the car door and stepped out. "Okay, here goes."

As a volunteer, I'd led a weekly Bible study for the residents of the homeless shelter for four years. This Christmas season, we were celebrating Advent, and had already lit the candles for hope, peace, and love, and talked about what each of those candles represent. Tonight we planned to light the candle that symbolizes joy, and celebrate with a party.

I walked to the office and rang the bell. When the door opened, the light inside was a sharp contrast to the dark outside. Since the previous week, the soberness of homelessness had been replaced by the hubbub of Christmas excitement. A local youth group had decorated the living area and donated a Christmas feast. My senses were bombarded by the magical transformation.

Residents wore smiling faces as they scurried to set the holiday table. The aroma of ham baking in the oven tantalized my taste buds. Christmas music blared from an old boom box. Welcoming hands reached out to bring me inside.

Walking into the kitchen, I found the table laden with bowls full of steaming vegetables. Holding a place of prominence in the center of the table, pink and purple candles nestled among shiny evergreen leaves and red berries to form our Advent wreath.

Our motley crew consisted of eight women, one man, and eight boys and girls ranging in ages from six months to twelve years. Among those women was Ms. Shirley, resident grandmother to the group who was, at least for this evening, family.

"Here," Ms. Shirley said as she pulled out a chair for me, "sit down." They'd saved the chair at the head of the table for me. I was humbled to be treated like the guest of honor by those I'd come to serve.

Amidst happy chatter, children laughing, milk spilling, and all that goes along with a large family dinner, we ate our fill, and then cleared the table. We turned off the overhead lights, relit the purple candles for hope, peace, and love, and lit the pink candle for joy.

I opened my Bible to Romans and read about the God of hope filling us with all joy and peace so we might overflow with hope. I looked around and into eyes of those who had experienced illness, lost jobs, struggled with drug addictions, and even served jail time. They had filled their stomachs with food, but I could sense in them a deeper hunger for the things we'd read about: hope, love, peace, and joy.

"What is joy?" I asked.

Gail lifted her hand and shyly asked, "Are happiness and joy the same thing?"

Well," Joan said, "they feel the same."

We talked and decided that both happiness and joy lead to feelings of well-being and contentment.

"I wasn't happy when I lost my job," Gail said.

"I wasn't happy when I was in jail," Ms. Shirley added.

"I wasn't happy when..."

We could all recall a time in our lives when we hadn't been happy.

Happiness, we decided, can be fleeting. Faced with adversity, the contentment that happiness produces might be extinguished as quickly as the flames of snuffed-out candles.

"What about joy?" I asked. "Do we lose our joy when those same bad things happen?"

"I had joy in my soul even when I lost my job," Gail said. "I knew the Lord would take care of me."

"I felt Him with me while I was in jail," Ms. Shirley said. "It was the only way I made it through those days."

After much discussion, we agreed that true and lasting joy is experienced only when we have a relationship with the One whose birthday we celebrated that night. We talked about the verse from Romans and the important words, "as you trust Him" and "by the power of the Holy Spirit." Our conversation was a testament to true joy that abides in our souls even when we're down and out and happiness is illusive.

We stood to close in prayer, formed a circle, and held hands, while the reflection of the flames from the candles of hope, and peace, and love, and joy flickered on the kitchen walls. We thanked God for sending his Son into the world to save us from our sins, and for the gift of joy that we'd all experienced, even in our worst circumstances.

I raised my head and looked around at the face of each resident. I saw glimmers of hope for better times, expressions of peace that passes understanding, love that each one of us had for the other, and the joy we had acknowledged deep down in our souls.

We made our way into the living room, with the children running past the adults. This was the moment they'd waited for all evening. The old sofa and chairs quickly filled and the children sat on the floor around the Christmas tree.

I asked if there were any requests for Christmas carols.

" 'Jingle Bells!" shouted Jenny, a bright-eyed three-year-old.

We sang "Jingle Bells" and every carol we could think of.

"Any other requests?" I asked.

" 'Jingle Bells'!" Jenny shouted again.

We laughed and again sang "Jingle Bells."

"Who wants to open gifts?" I asked.

"I do, I do!" the children shouted in unison.

I passed out the presents, and the children made a quick job of tearing into their gifts. I observed that the small gifts meant as much to the adults as they did to the children.

Later, as I packed up my basket to leave, Ms. Shirley came over to me and said, "Thank you."

"Ms. Shirley, you are so welcome," I said. "I hope you enjoy it."

"I appreciate the shower gel, but I mean the gift we shared upstairs when we talked about Jesus' birth, and the joy he gives us no matter what our circumstances."

One by one, the other adults echoed Ms. Shirley's sentiments.

I thought about the fields of Bethlehem, where an angel of the Lord appeared to shepherds and told them about the good news that would cause great joy for all the people. The angel said, "Today in the town of David a Savior has been born to you; he is the Messiah, the Lord."

Two thousand years later, homeless men, women, and children heard the same good news, and despite their desperate situations, every heart was stirred with great joy, including mine.

With my hand on the doorknob, I glanced back into the bright, warm, festive living room, then pushed the door open and stepped out into darkness. As I walked to the car, my eyes were drawn upward, to the twinkling stars. In a divine moment, I realized that my heart had been transformed, and was now full of joy, as Ms. Shirley said, about Jesus' birth, and the joy he gives us no matter what our circumstances.

~ Susan Dollyhigh

The rest of the story…

Ms. Shirley came to The Shepherd's House hoping for a better life. When interviewed by the local newspaper she said, "I had a good life. I had everything I could think of, a nice house, family and a husband of 35 years. But we got divorced six years ago, and then I hit rock bottom."

She admitted that she had the wrong friends, made bad choices and two-and-a-half years after the divorce she was arrested and spent three months in jail. After her release, with the help of the homeless shelter, Ms. Shirley found a job, saved her money, and had a place to call home.

Most importantly, Ms. Shirley had counseling, and re-committed her life to Jesus.

The day she graduated from the shelter to an apartment was bittersweet for both Ms. Shirley and the staff. But she soon returned as a volunteer, and later as a part-time employee.

On June 2, 2010, Ms. Shirley once again graduated, this time to Heaven. It was another bittersweet day for her family and friends. But we take comfort in knowing we'll see her again real soon.

Ms. Shirley, I was honored to call you "friend." Susan

47

My After-Christmas Surprise

After Christmas, my dad phoned. "Your mom needs new shoes. Would you take her shopping?"

I'd rather not, I thought. With the hectic holidays just behind me, I felt relieved to stay away from shopping malls. But I loved Mom, and set a date.

Mom, in her mid-eighties, wasn't spry, so shopping with her would be slow. Since she didn't relish shopping or spending money, I expected this trip to be more of a necessity than a fun mother-daughter outing. Yet, throughout my childhood, Mom had always been patient while taking me shopping. Now the shoe was on the other foot (pun intended).

A few days later, I picked up Mom and drove to a nearby shopping mall. I parked close to the entrance so she wouldn't have far to walk. We shopped at several stores, where she tried on one pair of shoes after another. Finding comfortable shoes that suited her became a challenge.

"Remember those flashy red flats you bought me when I was a teen?" I asked.

"Yes, and what about those three-inch spiked heels you begged for?"

I laughed. "Too bad I can't buy you shoes like that." But those were not for her. Finally, Mom found a pair of basic black, low-heeled slip-ons that suited her. Package in hand, I took her arm, and we started back to the car. Along the way, we passed a yarn and stitchery shop holding an after-Christmas sale. On a discount table outside the store, I spied a crewel-embroidered Nativity scene framed in handsome walnut. It was identical to the one I had admired in my sister's home.

I had wanted to stitch one for myself but never found the time. Now the completed stitchery cost less than the original kit. I felt like God was smiling down on me and whispering, "I knew you wanted it and saved it just for you."

As we trudged to the car, weary from shopping, both of us carried parcels and wore contented smiles. I felt pleased that I could help Mom buy comfortable shoes she liked. It had turned out to be a pleasant mother-daughter time after all.

Later, admiring the detailed stitches on my new treasure, I realized if I hadn't taken Mom shopping, I wouldn't have found this bargain. While I was meeting the needs of my mother, God surprised me with a gift from above.

Mom doesn't wear her new shoes anymore. She doesn't need them in heaven. But each year as I hang my cherished Nativity in our home, I recall our special shopping trip and the sweet surprise of God's after-Christmas gift to me.

Every good and perfect gift is from above,
coming down from the Father of the heavenly lights.
James 1:17 (NIV)

~ Lydia E. Harris

❧ 48 ☙

Gregg's Christmas Eve

Not every Christmas Eve is happily celebrated.

The holiday season is a festive and memorable time for most people. But it can also be a depressing and vulnerable time for those without family members or who are single. For those who have lost loved ones during this celebratory time of year, it can be an especially excruciating reminder of their loss.

I'll never forget the Christmas Eve phone call I received three years ago. "He's gone, Nate – Gregg is gone."

Gregg and his wife were more than good neighbors. We became close friends as we shared many lawn-talks and meals. Lawn-talks are those impromptu conversations while standing in front lawns or hollering back and forth as we empty mailboxes after arriving home from work. We also enjoyed many cookouts and holiday meals together.

Three years ago in July, Gregg asked if my children and I would be interested in a trip to the beach. They had planned a family gathering and made the necessary reservations only to have some unexpected cancellations. As the fees were nonrefundable, it would be nice for them to recover some of their expense. Because the price was a fraction of the normal cost, it was an easy decision to spend time at the beach with friends and family.

The beach setting was beautiful as we immersed ourselves in the sand, surf, and sun. Relaxing on the beach and beside the pool have always been favorite family activities. Very few things can top a long walk down the beach – either during the heat of the day while dodging fellow beach walkers and joggers or at night with the moonlight shimmering off the waves.

But this trip was different.

While enjoying an evening meal together, Gregg shared something deeply personal. Tears moistened his eyes as he told me he had been diagnosed with a rare blood disorder. Without treatment, he didn't have much time left. With treatment he could possibly salvage five years or longer.

His medical treatment, which would start in October, would be at a university medical facility out of town and could last several months, so short term living arrangements were made. Gregg's wife would stay at home and continue working while visiting him as often as possible.

The morning Gregg left, I was walking down my driveway to place some mail in the mailbox. He saw me, waved, and then drove over to chat before leaving. Leaning down so I could look through the open passenger window, I wished him a safe trip and speedy recovery. He asked that I look in on his wife – and help her fix the downstairs toilet since the water in its tank ran continually.

This was the kind of man Gregg was – while facing treatment for a life-threatening illness, his main concern was for his wife.

I reassured him we'd take care of his toilet – that he needed to focus on getting well and back to us. Little did I know, it would be our last conversation. If I had it to do all over again, I wouldn't waste time on toilet talk – I would focus on what is truly important. And I would have prayed with him.

I had surgery in mid-November and became preoccupied with my own recovery process, bouncing between physical therapy sessions and follow-up doctor appointments. Initially, Gregg and I planned to take care of each other's lawn while the other was recovering. So he was supposed to have been well by then. But life doesn't always work out as planned.

Just before Thanksgiving, Gregg's wife updated me on his worsening situation. Numerous medications prescribed to treat his illness created severe side effects. To address those side effects, more medications were prescribed. His condition slowly deteriorated as all these chemicals burned through him.

Gregg's body finally gave out and he passed into eternity on Christmas Eve in 2011.

Year-end activities hold new meaning for me. As families gather around fireplaces or dinner tables, I remember a dear friend who is sorely missed. Sure, I miss his insight on having and maintaining the perfect lawn. But I also miss his big smile and infectious laughter. I miss his loving dedication and intense affection for his wife. I miss his friendship.

Each year during the holidays, I honor his memory by remembering him and being grateful for the privilege of having known him. In his own way, God used my brief final visit with Gregg to change me. I reflect on eternity often. I am more mindful of the shortness of this precious earthly life. I am more willing to pray with people who are facing hardships. I am also more aware of the hollow loneliness experienced by those who have lost loved ones during the year.

I hope and pray this holiday season is filled with happiness and joy as you gather with family and friends. But amidst all the tinsel, wrapping paper, decorations, and meals, I urge you not to take your loved ones for granted. Tell them how much they mean to you. Invest in them while you can. Pray with them. Hug them. Encourage them. Make each holiday season the best one ever – you never know which could be the last.

– Nate Stevens

ॐ 49 ॐ

The First Christmas Without Dad

Bob and I took care to establish traditions that would ensure that Christmas was the best holiday of the year for our family – one of the more unusual of those traditions being that someone in our family always got a box of dirt. Never mind the significance. It was just part of what it meant to be a Whitson. But as my four children (ages twenty-one, eighteen, fifteen, and twelve) and I faced Christmas 2001, no one cared about the box of dirt. Dad had died of cancer the previous February.

We had known for months that he was going to die and we had always believed that when he did, he would take up residence in heaven – the ultimate graduation, if one chose to look at it that way. We would see him again. God's promise was sure. But knowing that didn't spare us the pain of facing that first Christmas without him.

Grief is a strange journey. Sometimes it leads us straight at the thing we dread, and we face it down. Sometimes we need to take a detour, to avoid the dreaded thing until we are stronger.

As Christmas approached, I felt we all needed the detour. A phone call provided it, but it took me a few days to embrace it.

A dear niece had been living and working in Geneva, Switzerland, for two years. Was there any way the children and I could spend Christmas with her?

No, I didn't think so.

Maybe.

I would get back to her.

At the last minute I asked something absurd. If we came to Geneva, did she think we might also be able to spend a few days in Paris? I'd lived in France when I was in college, and I had always longed to return.

Laura didn't hesitate. Of course! It would be great fun. Just let her know.

She'd see what she could do about finding hotel deals.

I hung up and contemplated the obstacles. My two oldest children had jobs. They wouldn't be able to get away. They were both in love. They wouldn't want to leave for a week at Christmas.

And the money. Oh, the money.

As it turned out, the airfare was miraculously cheap. The two oldest children wanted to go. Their bosses let them off. My financial advisor approved. Bob would approve, he said. I thought he was probably right. And so, on Christmas Eve, instead of crying our way through the usual, we were on our way to Geneva. On Christmas Day, instead of stumbling into the Daddy-less living room and pretending to enjoy opening presents, we were fighting jet lag, walking the medieval streets of Geneva, and eating dinner with an international group of Laura's friends from Switzerland, Sweden, and England. My Midwestern children loved it.

The day after Christmas we boarded the TGV and sped to Paris. I speak French and I adore Paris. This part of my life predated my falling in love with their father. There were no sad memories to confront here. I couldn't wait to share Paris with my children. Would they "get it"?

Standing before Notre Dame Cathedral, my son asked, "When did you say they built that?"

"In the 1200s."

He stepped closer to the doors, staring up and up and up at the myriad stone carvings.

Wow!

One night we rode the metro, emerging along the Seine, admiring a particularly beautiful bridge and watching an excursion boat make its way up the river before advancing beyond the row of trees shading the walkway. The Eiffel Tower loomed above us in the night, its ironwork glowing bronze in the lights.

Wow!

On another night we read the sign mounted on a tall iron fence not far from our hotel near the Sorbonne and discovered we'd been casually walking past the third-century ruins of a Roman bath. Roman. As in Julius Caesar and togas.

Wow!

We grabbed floor plans of the Louvre one day just before it closed, and that evening in our hotel room I told the children to look it over and mark the three things they most wanted to see. I wanted them to see less and appreciate more — to remember more than a maze of marbled halls.

The next morning at the museum, I watched my children watch. What would they really see? It turned out to be the Greek/Roman/Italian sculpture. My children were in awe. Their mother was delighted. They were getting it... they really were getting it.

In those four days, we probably walked five miles a day. We didn't see the Musee d'Orsay or go up the Eiffel Tower or ride on an excursion boat or eat at a fancy restaurant or do any number of a zillion things tourists usually go to Paris to see and do. We did, however, climb the towers of Notre Dame and see the gargoyles. We walked the streets of Little Athens and marveled over the array of foods. We shopped at the century old La Samaritaine department store. We ate mussels and crepes and lychees, discovered Nutella, and marveled at the smallness of the cars and the beauty of the roses at a flower market. We made mistakes and we got lost.

I don't imagine I'll ever spend Christmas in Paris again. But in 2001, travelling far, far away from home helped one heartbroken family detour around a monster named Grief. We spent our first Christmas without Dad in the City of Lights. Of course, Dad spent the day with the One who said, "Let there be light." But we did all right, too, because we came home knowing that we were going to be all right. We would return to the beloved traditions the next Christmas, and we would smile through our tears when the lucky recipient opened that box of dirt.

~ Stephanie Grace Whitson

❧ 50 ❧

Small Things

January! A new year. A time of new beginnings.

That gives some people an incentive to start over, turn over a new leaf, make resolutions. Others have tried that and failed so often the idea is daunting. Why bother?

We know Scripture says, "I can do all things through Christ, who gives me strength."

I don't argue with that. I know Jesus can do things perfectly, but I either can't or don't do my part. Sometimes other things get in the way of my goals.

The negative thought occurred to me that "I can only do Small Things."

Yet, the more I thought about it, the more I realized that just may be the answer to times of anxiety, feeling…dejected, depressed, like a failure and what's-the-use-of-trying.

Luke 16:10 tells us he who is faithful in little will be faithful in much.

We are admonished to grow in faith – grow in our Christian walk.

Maybe I'll never be the most popular, the most intelligent, the most successful. But I can love.

What did Jesus say? "Love one another."

What did Paul write? "There are three things: faith, hope and love. The greatest is love."

Love is…great? Not small?

Then yes, I can do something great. I can love.

We might say, "Well, those around me aren't that lovable."

What is love? I've always heard that "love is action." A fine preacher said it this way: "Love your way to feeling."

I like what Jeanne Bice said: "No one can make a brand new start. Anyone can start from now and make a brand new ending."

And that can be done anytime – not just in January.

So, although I'm working on my resolutions, and did take enough stuff out of my closet to turn it into a Prayer Closet for those most burdensome prayers, I want to make a different resolution: Start making a brand new ending.

Love is a small thing to do. But it's so great.

~ *Yvonne Lehman*

The Christmas season ends. Bills come. This remains:

> *God so loved the world*
> *that he gave his only begotten Son,*
> *so that whoever believes in him shall not perish,*
> *but have everlasting life.*
> John 3:16 (NASB)

About the Authors

Hannah Alexander is the pen name for husband-wife writing team Mel and Cheryl Hodde. Mel, a physician, provides medical wisdom and editing for Cheryl's novels. They write women's romantic medical fiction with small-town settings, and have worked together for twenty years. "A Christmas Lesson" is Cheryl's story.

Max Elliott Anderson uses his extensive experience in dramatic film, video, and television commercial production to bring that same visual excitement, and heart-pounding action to his many adventures and mysteries for middle grade readers eight-years-old and older. You can visit his *Books for Boys Blog* at http://booksandboys.blogspot.com, or his Amazon Author Page at http://www.amazon.com/Max-Elliot-Anderson/e/B002BLP3EE.

David Knox Barker is a writer and entrepreneur. He is the founder of ALP Life Sciences, the distributor of the Omega 3 supplement ALP High 3. ALP is also managing the Nanoveson research project, playing its role in the quest for treatment of chronic inflammatory diseases, including heart disease, cancer, diabetes, arthritis and many others. For more information visit: https://www.ALPLifeSciences.com.

Penny A. Bragg spent the majority of her professional career in the California public school system as a teacher, principal, and district administrator. Through the miraculous reconciliation of her marriage after an eleven-year divorce, God led Penny and her husband, Clint, into fulltime ministry in 2006. Together, they serve as marriage missionaries – sharing their testimony of restoration across the nation and abroad. Through Inverse Ministries, their non-profit organization, Penny also ministers to those who have experienced traumatic loss. Visit her blog at www.ForThoseWhoWeep.com.

Gary L. Breezeel is a former attorney, minister, and government accountant. After retiring in 2009, Gary moved to Arkansas with his wife of more than forty years to be closer to his grandchildren. Soon after, he joined White County Creative Writers to learn how to be a better writer. He writes mostly short stories and has won a number of writing awards in the area. He assists in a local ministry that helps the chronically unemployed find and keep jobs. In his spare time he enjoys reading as well as attending sports and other activities involving his grandchildren.

Joann Claypoole is the author of *DoveStories,* a children's chapter book series for ages six-eight. *The Gardener's Helpers* (Morgan James Publishing) is scheduled for release in late 2014. She has written a children's devotional book, *Coo Says You Are Loved* for ages two through five. Her story, "A Picture in the Sky", is included in *Divine Moments* (Grace Publishing). Joann co-wrote the script *My Last Hope* for a TV documentary hosted by Candace Cameron Bure and produced by National House of Hope. Her inspirational prayers have been featured on Clickandpray.com and have been compiled into two books, *All I Am* and *Everything to Me.* She writes songs, voiceovers, plays, articles, and blogs. Joann is a member of the Christian Writers Guild, Word Weavers Orlando chapter, and SCBWI. She is a wife, mother of four sons, Numi to three grandbabies, doggie-mom of two, and salon/spa owner in sunny Florida. Joann serves local and international missions and loves to sing on the praise and worship leading team at her local church.

Susan Shelton Dollyhigh is a freelance writer and speaker. She is a contributing author in *Spirit and Heart: A Devotional Journey; Faith and Finances: In God We Trust; The Ultimate Christian Living; God Still Meets Needs;* and *I Believe in Heaven* with Cecil Murphey and Twila Belk. Susan's articles have appeared in *Connection Magazine, Exemplify Magazine, Mustard Seed Ministry, P31 Woman, The Upper Room* and *The Secret Place.*

Janice S. Garey lives in Atlanta with husband Art, and Miss Bosley, a stray kitten who arrived for Christmas 2013 in a divine moment. Janice's publishing credits include book reviews, an article in *Church Libraries,* and an article in the *Christian Library International* (CLI) newsletter about the need for Spanish language Bibles in prisons. She loves co-teaching first through sixth grade Sunday school, and treasures Women's Missionary Union relationships. She takes writing courses with Christian Writers Guild. As a CLI volunteer she hopes to reach prisoners and the world with God's word.

Tommy Scott Gilmore, III, a gifted speaker and motivational leader, is Executive Director of Changing Lives Ministry in Asheville, NC. His life has not been boring. To experience poverty, he spent a winter's month in Boston's ghetto with only fifty cents in his pocket. He rode a bicycle over 20,000 miles through 20 states and 12 countries, climbed St. Goddard Pass in the Swiss Alps, and cheated death on several occasions. He survived quicksand, numerous auto accidents and threats on his life from his preaching. You can find his life-changing testimony on his website: www.ChangingLivesMinistry.Info.

Gail Griner Golden is an experienced blogger, artist, and author of many inspirational articles, poems, and devotionals. She has been published in newspapers and Christian magazines including *Christianity Today*, *The Upper Room*, and *Evangel*. Gail and her husband, Rabbi Jem Golden, minister together at Ma'gen Da'vid Messianic Synagogue in Port St. John, Florida. She enjoys teaching the Torah, and the Jewish roots of Christianity through the synagogue as well as through her blog, Gail-Friends (www.gailgolden.org).

Gigi Graham is the eldest daughter of Ruth and Billy Graham. She is married and the mother of seven grown children, grandmother to nineteen grandchildren – so far – and one great grandson. Gigi's experience as the daughter of a well-known evangelist, raising seven children, living in both the Middle East and Europe, has given her many resources for her writing and speaking ministry. She serves as Ambassador of the Billy Graham Training Center at The Cove in Asheville, North Carolina. Gigi is an award-winning author of several books including *Weather of the Heart, Currents of the Heart* and *A Quest for Serenity*. She divides her time between central Florida and the mountains of North Carolina and can be contacted through Ambassador Agency in Nashville, Tennessee.

Lydia E. Harris has been married to her college sweetheart, Milt, for forty-seven years. They have two married children and five grandchildren ranging from preschool to high school. Lydia earned a Master of Arts degree in home economics. She has written numerous articles, book reviews, devotionals, and stories. Focus on the Family's Clubhouse magazine for children publishes her recipes, which she develops and tests with her grandchildren. She writes the column, "A Cup of Tea with Lydia," and is called Grandma Tea by her grandchildren. Lydia has contributed to numerous books and is author of the book, *Preparing My Heart for Grandparenting: For Grandparents at Any Stage of the Journey* (AMG Publishers).

Lillian Humphries has been successfully writing articles in her newsletters for a ladies ministry. She is currently writing a contemporary Christian romance novel. You can connect with her at http://connectedchristianwomen.blogspot.com; Lillian Tamanini Humphries on Facebook; or Lillian Humphries on Twitter.

John Kincaid and his wife Kathy have two children. John grew up in church, and received Christ at age twelve. They are members of North Hills Community Church in Taylors, South Carolina where they work with

Operation Christmas Child. John has taught adult Sunday school and Bible studies since 1985, and leads a prison ministry. In previous churches, John sang in choir, worked with children and youth, and served on mission trips. He writes a daily devotional for the website http://changinglivesministry.info.

Alice Klies is a freelance writer and member of Northern Arizona's Word Weavers International and has been published in *WordSmith Journal*. Her stories, "Just Us Girls" and "The Dog Did What?" are published in *Chicken Soup for the Soul*. Other stories appearing in anthologies include "Grandfather, Father and Me," "Grandmother, Mother and Me," "God Still Meets Needs," and "Friends of Faith." Still another, "Angels on Earth" is published in *Guideposts*. Alice is currently writing a memoir.

Yvonne Lehman is author of over 50 novels. She founded, and for 25 years directed the Blue Ridge Mountains Christian Writers Conference, and now directs the Blue Ridge Novelist Retreat held annually in October at the Ridgecrest North Carolina conference center. She lives in panoramic Black Mountain North Carolina with her beautiful, furry blond and white Pomeranian, Rigel, named after a Titanic survivor. Her latest books are *Finding Love in South Carolina* book #1 and book #2, *Finding Love in North Carolina* book #1 and book #2 (Greenbrier – 2 novels in each book), *The Reluctant Schoolmarm* in *Reluctant Brides* collection (Barbour), *Crashing into Christmas* (Lighthouse Publishing of the Carolinas), and *Divine Moments* (Grace Publishing). Her 50th book is *Hearts that Survive – A Novel of the Titanic* (Abingdon Press). She blogs with *ChristiansRead* and *Novel Rocket*.

Delores Liesner, whether writing, speaking, or as God's delivery girl, lives life passionately and humorously revealing dynamic hope and confidence found in the heritage of our personal God. She writes from Racine, Wisconsin, is a CLASS graduate, and has published hundreds of stories, devotionals and articles. As columnist, writer and teacher, Delores is represented by Linda Glaz of Hartline Literary Agency. Contact her at http://deloresliesner.com or delores7faith@yahoo.com. Delores' writing supports the Fullness of Life Foundation, which raises funds for treatment expenses for children with life-threatening illness.

Lori Marett and her husband, Rodney, have directed the annual Gideon Media Conference & Film Festival for seven years. Her screenwriting career began two decades ago when she won and/or was finalist for many regional and national screenplay contests, which opened the door for her to adapt producer

Ken Wales' *Sea of Glory* for the screen. She co-wrote her first feature film, *Meant to Be* with producer/director Bradley Dorsey in December 2012. She adapted Jenny L. Cote's novel, *The Ark, the Reed, and the Fire Cloud* into a screenplay for an animated feature film and an animated television series. Lori has several articles published including "Smell the Flowers" in *Divine Moments*. Lori lives with her three daughters in Black Mountain, North Carolina while her husband does contract medical/security work in Afghanistan.

Dr. Julie Hale Maschhoff, a retired professor from Illinois State University, has been published in *Penned from the Heart*, *Mature Years*, and *Dialogue Magazine*. She also collaborated on a parenting video series for Learning Seed. Her women's Bible study, *Golden Fruit* was published by Concordia Publishing House. Julie is a member of Treasure Coast Word Weavers International. She and her husband are enjoying retirement in the beautiful state of Florida where they reside with Julie's service dog, Spartacus.

Edie Melson is the author of four books, including *Fighting Fear: Winning the War at Home When Your Soldier Leaves for Battle*. She's also the military family blogger for *Guideposts* at *While They Serve*. Her popular blog for writers, *The Write Conversation,* reaches thousands each month, and she's the co-director of the Blue Ridge Mountains Christian Writers Conference. *Connections: Social Media & Networking Techniques for Writers* is a print expansion of her bestselling ebook on social media. She's the Social Media Mentor at *My Book Therapy*, the Social Media Director for *Southern Writers Magazine*, as well as the Senior Editor for NovelRocket.com. Connect on Twitter and Facebook.

Sharon J. Morris is an MK (Missionary Kid) from Indonesia. She has been married to Donald D. Morris, II for thirty years. They have two adult children, Othella Rose and DJ. Sharon is working on a memoir about her experiences as an MK and has self-published an inductive Bible Study titled *Worshiping God*. She has been a member of Word Weavers for several years.

Vicki H. Moss is Contributing Editor for *Southern Writers Magazine* and past Editor-at-Large for two years. A columnist for *American Daily Herald*, she's also a poet, author of *How to Write for Kids' Magazines* and *Writing with Voice*, a Precept Ministries leader and a Christian Communicators graduate. She has written for *Hopscotch* and *Boy's Quest* magazines for the last decade. She's also published in *Divine Moments* (Grace Publishing), *SouthWest Sage, Country Woman, In the City, Borderlines,* Scotland's *Thistle Blower,* and *I Believe In Heaven* by Cecil Murphey and Twila Belk. Selected to be a presenter of her fiction and creative nonfiction short stories for three conferences in a row at the Southern Women Writers Conference held at Rome, Georgia's Berry College, Vicki, also a speaker, is on faculty for various writers conferences. Learn more at http://www.livingwaterfiction.com

Kimberly Pickens writes to bring God glory and prays that others are blessed and uplifted by her stories. She lives in Simpsonville, South Carolina with her husband, nine-year-old son and what she describes as her spoiled-rotten dog. Her daughter is a college sophomore. She has a passion to write and share God's mercy and goodness. She attends the writing chapters of American Christian Fiction Writers and Crosses & Pens. Her writing won an honorable mention that was submitted to First Five Pages Contest. This is her first published article.

Deborah Raney's first novel, *A Vow to Cherish*, inspired the film of the same title and launched Deb's writing career. Twenty years, thirty books, and numerous awards later, she's still writing. She and husband, Ken, recently traded small-town life in Kansas – the setting of many of Deb's novels – for life in the city of Wichita. They love traveling to visit five (so far) grandchildren, and their four children, who are all grown now, and having snowflake parties with their own children.

Colleen L. Reece describes herself as an ordinary person with an extraordinary God. Raised in a home without electricity or running water but filled with love for God and family, Colleen learned to read by kerosene lamplight and dreamed of someday writing a book. God had multiplied her "someday" book into *150 Books You Can Trust*, with six million copies sold.

Linda Wood Rondeau is a multi-published author. Her debut novel, *The Other Side of Darkness* (Pelican Book Group) won the 2012 Selah Award in that category. Linda has followed that book up with a second award-winning book, *A Christmas Prayer*, also titled, *A Father's Prayer* (Lighthouse Publishing of the Carolinas). Other works include: *Joy Comes to Dinsmore Street*, *Days of Vines and Roses*, and *I Prayed for Patience: God Gave Me Children* (Helping Hands Press) as well as her Christmas favorite, *It Really IS a Wonderful Life* (LPC). A former resident of the Adirondack area, Linda now resides in Jacksonville, Florida with her still very patient husband Steve. Read more at www.lindarondeau.com.

Toni Armstrong Sample retired from Pennsylvania to South Carolina at the end of a successful career as a Human Resource Executive, and owner of a management consulting, training, and development firm. A published author in journals and magazines, she celebrates the 2014 release of her first three novels of inspiration, intrigue and romance, *The Glass Divider, Transparent Web of Dreams,* and *Distortion.* Toni is a Christian retreat leader, conference speaker, Bible study facilitator, and commission artist.

Sherry Schumann, having traveled along a journey of healing and redemption, proclaims her greatest joy is the Lord. She leads women's Bible studies and co-chairs a community James 1:27 team. Her wildlife photography from the South Carolina Lowcountry is featured at women's prayer and healing services. She and her husband are blessed with three sons, two daughters-in-law, and an adorable granddaughter. Sherry's first novel, *The Christmas Bracelet,* was published by WestBow Press. She also published an Easter drama, *They Knew No Easter,* by Lillenas.

Nate Stevens is a missionary kid who grew up in a Christian home and church. He has enjoyed a thirty-year banking career in a variety of leadership roles. He writes online devotions for Christian Devotions Ministries, devotions for his home church, Calvary Church in Charlotte, North Carolina, and articles for several publications. His book, *Matched 4 Marriage – Meant 4 Life* is available at major book retailers. His next book, *Deck Time in the Storm,* is currently in production. He speaks at conferences, seminars and Bible study groups for singles, young adults, young marrieds, and youth. He lives near Charlotte, North Carolina and is an active dad with his two awesome kids, Melissa and Mitchell. Find contact and book information at http://www.natestevens.net.

Fran Lee Strickland is writing her first romantic suspense novel, *The Message of the Stone Tree,* and is designing a blog so she can connect with friends and readers. She works full time as chief financial officer for the City of Abbeville, South Carolina, serves as treasurer of American Christian Writers of Upstate South Carolina, American Christian Fiction Writers Chapter of South Carolina, and is a member of Blue Ridge Writers group based near Asheville, North Carolina. Fran is a single mother of one son, Jake, who drives a monster truck that makes a lot of noise and blows a lot of smoke. She loves to try new recipes, has eclectic tastes in music, and drinks more coffee than she should. Visit her blog at http://www.scatteringwordsandsowingseeds.blogspot.com

Ann Tatlock is a two-time winner of the major Christy Award. She has also won the Midwest Independent Publishers Association Book of the Year in fiction for *All the Way Home* and *I'll Watch the Moon. Publishers Weekly* calls her "one of Christian fiction's better wordsmiths." Ann lives with her husband and daughter in Asheville, North Carolina.

Stephanie Grace Whitson a best-selling, award-winning author celebrated her twentieth anniversary as a published Christian novelist in 2014. She has a Master of Arts degree in history and is a frequent guest speaker/lecturer on a variety of historical and inspirational topics for both civic organizations and church groups. Her husband and blended family, her church, historical research, antique quilts, and Kitty – her motorcycle – all rank high on her list of "favorite things." Learn more at www.stephaniewhitson.com.

Eric Wiggin grew up with his parents, grandparents and six siblings on a farm on the edge of the Maine wilderness, where they grew and canned their own food, lighted with kerosene lamps and heated with wood. Eric now lives with his wife Dot in rural Michigan, where they raise a large garden and heat with wood. Eric and Dot are the parents of four adult children, twelve grandchildren and three great-grandchildren. Eric has been a pastor, schoolteacher and college instructor. He is the author of *The Gift of Grandparenting* (Focus on the Family) and seventeen novels for young adults and adults, both in paper and for Kindle.

Dr. Rhett H. Wilson, Sr., pastors The Spring Church in Laurens, South Carolina. He enjoys life with his wife Tracey and their three children, Hendrix, Anna-Frances, and Dawson. The Wilsons explore waterfalls in the Carolinas, tube down mountain streams, and look forward to March Madness basketball each year. Rhett likes reading legal thrillers and Southern fiction, writing, and listening to country, classical, and Broadway music. Rhett and Tracey have released two CDs, *Lead Me On* and *Offered Praises*. He is writing a book titled *Seven Words to Pray for My Family*. Rhett is available to speak or sing at your church. Visit his blog, *Faith, Family, and Friends*, at www.rhettwilson.blogspot.com.

www.ingramcontent.com/pod-product-compliance
Lightning Source LLC
Chambersburg PA
CBHW071313110426
42743CB00042B/1558